HAND IN HAND

Copyright © 1992 by Fund Raising Institute

Published by
Fund Raising Institute
A Division of The Taft Group
12300 Twinbrook Parkway, Suite 450
Rockville, Maryland 20852
(301) 816-0210

Printed in the United States of America

97   96   95   94   93   92   6   5   4   3   2   1

Library of Congress Catalog Card Number: T/K
ISBN 0-930807-37-5

Fund Raising Institute publishes books on fund raising, philanthropy, and
nonprofit management. To request sales information, or a copy of our catalog,
please write us at the above address or call 1-800-877-TAFT.

The paper used in this publication meets the minimum requirements
of American National Standard for Information Sciences—Permanence
Paper for Printed Library Materials, ANSI Z39.48-1984.   ∞™

I dedicate this book to my wife, Anne; my mother, June; and my late father, William, whose support over the years has given me a chance to give something back to the world.

And, in memory of my two friends and fund-raising colleagues, Ray Weiss and Bob Hanna, who died before the completion of a capital campaign that would not have been successful without them.

Contents

Acknowledgments

I would not have been able to write this book without the help and support of Goldie K. Alvis, Cleveland Foundation; Dr. Ralph Brody, Federation for Community Planning (Cleveland); Morris Everett, Jr., CFRE, Morris Everett & Associates; Evelyn Croft Faulkner, CFRE, American Red Cross; Lynne Feighan, Laurel School; Michael Haggerty, Gail Holocker, and John Hannon, Parmadale; Susan Golden, CFRE, The Golden Group; James Hardie, consultant; Paul Kantz, John Carroll University; Anne E. Mengerink, M.S.S.A., Parmadale; David Mikolajczyk, Parmadale; Karen Owens, Resource Development Network; Patricia Pasqual, Foundation Center—Cleveland; Patricia Scalzi, Case Western Reserve University; Jay Seaton, Bank One; Janet Shipman, United Way Services; Sr. Joan L. Sustersic, OP, Parmadale; and David Twining.

I owe a special thanks to Bruce Mack and Thomas Konkoly, CFRE, from Baldwin-Wallace University, for their help with the planned giving.

I am deeply grateful to Thomas W. Woll, not only for his longtime support and friendship but also for his brilliant leadership of Parmadale which, for many children, is the only chance they have.

HAND IN HAND

Funding Strategies
for Human Service Agencies

WILLIAM C. MENGERINK, CFRE

FUND RAISING INSTITUTE
A Division of The Taft Group
Rockville, Maryland

Introduction

This book is designed to help small to midsize human and social service agencies improve their ability to raise money. I have made four assumptions about those who will benefit most from reading it.

The first assumption is that the reader has scarce resources. If you have enough money to afford fund-raising and public relations staff, sophisticated computer systems, consultants, and four-color printed materials, this book may not be for you. If, instead, your last fund-raising action plan was written on a napkin over lunch with the only member of the board who is mildly interested in the subject and you can't even find the napkin, this book should help you.

The second assumption is that the reader is either a director of an agency, responsible for much more than fund raising, or a one-person development office. If you have more support than this, all the better. This book will be a useful resource, though, for board members as well as directors and fund-raising staff members.

The third assumption I made is that your agency provides quality services to people who need them. If you don't, the principles and practices described here won't work.

And, the fourth assumption is that you are service-driven. All nonprofits, of course, provide some service. My experience has been, however, that workers in human and social services have been especially singular in their zeal to achieve their service and program objectives. Although this characteristic has been an asset, it has been a limitation for some to the extent that it has inhibited their growth in the relatively new frontier of fund raising.

The critical elements of a good fund-raising program are identified in the first chapter and discussed in detail in later chapters. I believe that you will benefit from reading the entire book in sequence. However, each chapter has been designed to stand alone so that you can choose to focus on the areas in which you are most interested.

1 Creating a Strong Fund-Raising Organization

There is no cause half so sacred as the cause of a people.
There is no idea so uplifting as the idea of the service of
humanity.

—Woodrow Wilson

Ten years ago, most of us didn't even know the vocabulary of fund raising let alone the intricate types of relationships and techniques used by colleges and cultural organizations that have been raising money since, it seems, the Renaissance.

Human and social services agencies were traditionally organized to deliver services to people in need. As directors, over the years, we continued to keep our eyes on our clients or budgets and our budgets were fat with government funding. Those times might have been good, but those times are gone.

This chapter describes the small but vital changes in board relationships, lines of communication, policies, and procedures needed to create the arena in which successful fund raising can occur.

You may have seen the television commercial where a voice-over promises the viewer that he, too, can make a million dollars in real estate. *You, too, can make a million dollars in real estate!* the voice shouts. Then, an excited announcer steps in front of the camera and says something like, "O.K.! O.K! How do you make a million dollars in real estate? How? *First*, you buy a high-rise apartment . . ."

Similarly, when human and social service agencies try to recover some of their lost government funding by replicating the fund raising done in larger organizations with long fund-raising histories, it seems that our instructions have been, "O.K. First, you hire four secretaries, three assistants, two directors . . ." You know, or suspect, that it takes money to make money, but you simply don't have anywhere to take it from.

When I started fund raising in 1977, I had an old Royal typewriter, my own clock radio, a few hundred flyers containing 9,000 words printed so tiny that all anyone could read were the headings, a recently purchased salmon-colored suit (my favorite), and a volunteer steel plant foreman who knew less about fund raising than I did and I didn't know anything.

I learned a question very basic to fund raising, though, a question that applies to all fund-raising agencies. It was:

What do we absolutely have to do to successfully raise funds and how can we do it on a modest budget and with scarce staff resources?

I also learned that the answer to this question can be found in hard work, time, volunteers, and talent. These qualities form the basis of the following critical components of fund raising in our agencies.

The critical components of fund raising

1. *Elevate fund raising in your agency to a more prestigious status than it is now.* Those of you who have already made this transition know this means a change of attitude from, "I hate

this but somebody's gotta do it" to "This isn't as bad as I thought" and, finally, to "This is actually kind of fun . . ." If you are already enjoying fund raising, congratulations and keep up the good work.

Too often, though, fund raising is seen as a necessary evil, pushed to a back burner until the next financial crisis, and engaged in reluctantly at best and kicking and screaming at worst. The approach-avoidance associated with fund raising comes from a combination of the public knowledge that things aren't going to get any better on their own and the private opinion that fund raising is the product of charlatans or carnival barkers.

I predict that if you are patient, work hard, and apply the principles and practices in this book, you will not only raise more money but you will also start to enjoy fund raising. I also predict that you will be happy to learn that the development field is filled with people who value ethics and integrity. Professional fund raising is not a contradiction in terms.

2. *If you don't have the budget to hire an experienced and successful fund raiser, seek talent.* Although this may appear obvious, the point is that some of us, who are unable to afford a proven commodity in the field, will look for someone with as much experience as our limited budgets can attract. Given this handicap, I much prefer hiring people who are bright and talented and a *blank sheet* with regard to fund raising as long as they are hungry to learn. Recent college graduates with no experience, mid-life women reentering the job market after raising children, and retired people are good resources.

3. *Do an internal needs assessment.* When I read a book on fund raising, I usually do a "yeah, right" when I see a point about "needs assessment," "mission" or "agency goals" right at the beginning. In other words, I am anxious for the writer to get to the good part, the actual techniques. Suspecting that you may be going, "yeah, right," I need to say that it is very important for

you to know as specifically and clearly as possible what your needs are before you develop fund-raising methods.

The needs assessment should be done as part of an overall agency strategic planning process. Assess where you have been, where you are now, and where you want to be in the short term (one-two years), intermediate term (three-five years) and long term (six-ten years). Considering your current and future plans for programs and services, identify your financial needs for the short, intermediate and long terms. How much money will you need in the future for capital projects? How much unrestricted money for operations? How much for equipment or materials? When do you need it? What is most important?

Your needs assessment will form the foundation for your *case statement*, which describes the problems or needs of the clients you are trying to serve. This statement should always be expressed in terms of your client's needs rather than your own. As a donor, I may be interested in helping a blind child learn to use a special computer keyboard, but I'm not interested in knowing that the ABC Agency has had a rough year and doesn't have the money to purchase all the special equipment it needs. I may be moved by the need for mentally retarded adults to receive more specialized job training, but I don't care about the XYZ Agency that has to cut the number of its job trainers because of reduced government funding. Frame your case around the client's needs, rather than your own. These needs are your contact point with potential donors.

Also, write your case statement so that your board volunteers can learn it and "talk" it. As agency directors, we have become very articulate from years of experience making our case to the public. Your case statement, or a variation of it, will act as a script for your volunteers to begin to feel more comfortable selling your services to their colleagues and friends.

4. *Conduct an internal audit of your development office.* See Appendix A for a checklist of the essentials.

5. *Write a fund-raising action plan.* This plan should be

written clearly and include your needs, objectives, methods, budget, and timetable. Distribute it to all staff and board members involved in fund raising.

Review the plan regularly. However, remain open to *opportunistic decision making* as you go along. This means you can change your mind the day after you mail the final plan to everyone. The point is to see your plan as a way to stay on target, not as a life sentence.

6. *The director and staff should meet once a week for at least one hour.* Although this may appear to be a relatively insignificant procedural suggestion, it is not. Meeting regularly will improve your communications, ensure continuity, and give you momentum. Meetings should be organized so you are convening often enough to keep everyone moving forward but not so often that no one has time to get any other work done. Keep minutes of your major decisions.

Without regularly scheduled development meetings with staff and volunteers, the law of entropy will let your fund-raising plans drift back into the inert state they were in when you began the process of change.

7. *If possible, assign space for your development meetings and storage of materials.* This, too, may seem insignificant, but it will go a long way toward elevating the fund raising in your agency. This isn't to suggest a walnut-paneled office and wet bar, but this doesn't mean a converted laundry room, either. Make space a priority.

8. *Begin to develop a volunteer base that can help you achieve your fund-raising and public relations goals.* Volunteers can be grouped in three classes:

   a. Board volunteers who will make gifts and help ask a few people for a lot of money;
   b. Nonboard volunteers who will ask a lot of people for a little bit of money; and,
   c. Volunteers who will become your arms and legs and help you with the considerable amount of minutiae that fund raising generates.

9. *Provide training for staff and volunteers.* Although it may not be obvious at the beginning, the true objective of training is less about having your staff and volunteers collect other people's ideas about fund raising and more about helping them gain confidence in their own capacity to think creatively and act confidently.

10. *Build your programs around your present strengths.* Development in those areas in which you are already strong will encourage you to develop more gradually those areas in which you need improvement.

11. To the extent you can, *build one part of your program at a time.* Take six months to put something in place. Don't try to put six to eight fund-raising programs into place in a three-month period. You'll be better off in the long run if you build your programs as slowly as you can afford to.[1]

12. Remember Murphy's Law. If something can go wrong, it will. *Give yourselves more time than you think you will need to complete projects.*

13. *Don't undertake anything that your organization isn't ready to sustain.* I made a mistake like this several years ago when I rented 5,000 names from a list broker in Chicago. We broke even and acquired about 90 new donors, donors who with a little cultivation would have netted us a few thousand dollars if we had had the resources to follow through. Because our organization was not ready to followup on this acquisition mailing, the new donors died on the vine.

14. As a rule of thumb, *try to build a program that is not personality-dependent. Instead, build one that will work effectively no matter who the players are.* Although a highly charismatic, energetic development director will provide inspiration and, possibly, results in the short run, this same director will come to doubt himself over time if those around him come to expect miracles. Remember that people cannot *always* do what they can *sometimes* do.

15. *Set realistic financial goals.* This is partially for your

staff's state of mind, but is most especially important for your volunteers. We can't afford to allow our volunteers to fail. Staff can tolerate failure better than volunteers can.

16. *If you have a development director (or a staff performing a development function), give him or her (or them) the opportunity to develop personal relationships with key board members.* This runs counter to common wisdom since staff have been normally insulated from our boards or used only as attendants when members needed something. If you have the advantage of a fund-raising staff, it is important to create a climate where this person can come to share the ownership of fund raising with you and board members. By not empowering your staff to interact directly with board members, you will reduce one of your most important fund-raising assets to a clerical/secretarial position.

17. *Donor confidentiality is as important as client confidentiality.* We are accustomed to government, legal, and moral constraints on disclosure of information about the clients we serve. Donor confidentiality should be valued as deeply. Gift histories and personal information gained through prospect and donor research should be shared on a *need to know* basis. This would usually include the director, development staff, book-keeper, board president, and chairperson of your development committee. You can make a case for board members of the development committee as well, assuming that you are rating prospects to determine how much money to ask them for, but don't share information beyond this.

18. *No matter who you are asking for what, you will need to develop a crisp and provocative case statement.* Your case statement should show credibility; indicate what your needs are; and be informative, passionate, and written so that your volunteers can integrate parts of the statement into their own repertoire.

19. *Whether your agency needs a* **change** *tune-up or a* **change** *overhaul, the key is that you are willing to become the* **change agent** *and subject your organization to the invariable by-product of change: stress.* Assuming that change is necessary, it is helpful

to remind those involved to ask themselves not, "What's the matter with me?" but, rather, "*Who's* the matter with me?" Relationships suffer when we are stressed.

20. *It helps to have these qualities to be successful in fund raising:*
   a. *Energy and drive* (the square peg actually *will* fit in the round hole if you push it hard enough)
   b. *Finesse* (it's much easier to fit it into a square hole)
   c. A *tolerance for ambiguity* (nothing ever seems to be over or for certain)
   d. A *capacity for forming good relationships* (up and down the social hierarchy)
   e. *Ego strength to handle disappointment and frustration* (yes, sometimes even we fail)
   f. *Creativity* (coloring outside the lines)
   g. *Endurance to work long hours* (in fact, to give new meaning to long hours)
   h. An *open mind to new ideas* (which is especially difficult when these new ideas are not our own)

21. *Strengthen your public relations activities.* This assumes that like most local human and social service agencies, you provide high-quality programs and have a very low profile in the community.

22. *Learn to handle the pressures of fund raising.* Chapter ten is designed to help us stay comparatively sane and healthy in this highly competitive arena.

23. *Develop your board.*

The techniques of fund raising

The following areas form the critical components of a solid fund-raising strategy. Each is described in detail in subsequent chapters:

1. *Volunteers*
2. *Major gifts program*

3. *Annual fund*
4. *Grant development*
5. *Wills and bequests program*
6. *Corporate philanthropy*
7. *Special events*
8. *Capital campaigns*

Of all the components necessary to create an organization that raises money effectively, the most important is an active, capable board.

2 How to Develop a Fund-Raising Board

No man is a fool who gives away what he cannot keep, to gain what he cannot lose.

—Unknown

For years we did very well in fund raising at Parmadale, a residential child treatment center in Cleveland. We did everything well except ask other people for money.

We had a strong grants program, conducted proactive public relations activities on a modest budget and relatively scarce staff resources, designed a growing annual direct mail campaign, and sponsored two outstanding special events—a formal dinner dance and a golf classic. We even began to take the first few steps toward the introduction of an aggressive wills and bequests program.

Our challenge, though, was to learn how to more effectively *ask other people, outright, for money.*

There are at least two reasons why this was difficult. One has to do with the people who have staffed human and social service agencies over the years and the other has to do with the traditional role of volunteers on human and social service agency boards.

The changing role of staff

To better understand the interior world of human service workers, we need to remember that many of the present top managers of agencies entered the field in the '60s or '70s with fire in their bellies. We were social activists who were more interested in Bob Dylan than Peter Drucker. In short, we wanted to change the world and we certainly didn't need any help from the establishment.

Over the years, we focused on programs and services. We could afford to do this, of course, because of the relative abundance of government and foundation funding available to the more clever and aggressive among us.

As leaders, we became adept and comfortable with asking for money from government sources largely because this "ask" really involved an *exchange*. We would provide progams and services in exchange for public funding.

Foundations were even easier. They were easier because we knew that they were in the business of giving away money. This kind of asking was not confrontational. Except for a tactical phone call or two, or, possibly an on-site-review, the business of asking for money was, and is, done through a thoughtfully written proposal.

We even got pretty good at asking individuals for money, but only in those situations that involved an exchange for *something*. We could sell raffle tickets in exchange for the chance of winning a few bucks or dinner tickets in exchange for a meal. We could even bring ourselves to ask people to join something more ethereal like a "friends of the agency" club where the only exchange was a donor's money for a membership card and free parking.

However, few of us learned to effectively and comfortably ask other individuals for money, face-to-face, when no *apparent* exchange is involved.

Faced with the major decrease of government funding in the

'80s and the consequent bombardment of proposals submitted to foundations, agencies are now trying to replicate the type of fund raising that colleges, universities, and cultural organizations have been doing very well for so long. And, unfortunately, without very good results.

One reason our results have not been as good as they could be is suggested by a rule of thumb in fund raising that says: *whoever asks another person for money should be someone who is difficult to say "no" to.* This is a problem because human service-minded people haven't been spending much time over the last 20 years developing relationships with people of wealth and power. We can ask our moms and dads and brothers and sisters and even our friends and colleagues for ten or, once in awhile, a hundred dollars. In other words, we can ask a lot of people for a little bit of money.

The problem is we can't raise much money this way.

It is when we ask ourselves, instead, how we can ask a few people for a lot of money that we actually hear the bad news: *we learn that we are easy to say no to.*

To raise more money, we are coming to recognize the need to develop professional relationships in a new world, a world of tuxedos and cocktail dresses. We are coming, also, to recognize that we not only have to ask people outright for money but also motivate them to ask other people for their money.

The changing role of the board

The historical *expectations* and *composition* of volunteer boards of human service agencies are primary factors that make it difficult to ask people for money.

Up until a few years ago, people who were asked to serve on a human services board were expected to give their "time and talent." They did not expect to have to also give their money. For the most part, they did not think it was *their* job to raise money. They thought it was *your* job.

In addition, our boards have been composed of such professionals as social workers, psychologists, psychiatrists, accountants, lawyers, teachers, and, possibly, an occasional business person or two. It is more important, though to recognize who has not been on our boards: wealthy people who are economically and socially powerful in our communities, that is, the power elite.

In the past, our board members accepted their positions without ever having been told that they would have to make financial contributions to our agencies or ask anyone else for money. In fact, it is very possible, even likely, that our board members have never been personally asked for a significant and outright gift of money (as opposed to being asked to buy a raffle ticket or attend a dinner dance) by anyone . . . ever.

If you have even suggested that a change is needed, they may have said something to the effect that they are giving their "wisdom and work" and then stare at their feet.

When you press them harder, they may suggest buying their way out of the problem by hiring a development director whose job it would be to raise money, which, of course, won't work either unless you hire a very wealthy and powerful development director . . .

So, given the relative inexperience of our staff and the composition and traditional expectations of our boards, where do we go from here? How do we develop a board that will become the center of all of our fund-raising activities?

The critical components of board development

1. *Come to realize, if you haven't already, that it is not a contradiction of terms for people who have wealth and power to also be interested in improving the quality of the lives of others.* If we still feel a twinge of self-betrayal when we attend an infrequent "high society" activity, we should try to change our point of view. How we *perceive* wealth and power will influence our

capacity to attract it. In fact, it may take awhile to become desensitized to even using the terms, "wealth" and "power."

In my salad days, in 1975, I wore jeans and a T-shirt and ran a cottage for 20 teenagers who were living at Parmadale. When my boss learned I could type, he gave me the job of Director of Research and Development. Neither of us really knew what that meant. I went to a clothing outlet and bought three suits for $60 and a cheap pair of wingtips. I didn't know a Gucci from a Poochie.

Ten years later, I found myself in a job where I not only needed to develop relationships with people who have much more money than I, but I have to try to convince them that they should give Parmadale a lot of it.

We need to learn that whether we like it or not there are a small number of people in each or our communities who control the economy and influence which organizations and agencies receive funding. Our awareness of this power structure, our ability to penetrate it and feel comfortable relating to people within it will improve our ability to raise funds.[1]

We need to learn to be comfortable not only in the work room but also the board room.

2. Few of us learned, in the 1980s, to ask other people for money when no exchange is involved. The truth is that their really is an exchange and all it takes is a shift in our attitudes to recognize and capitalize on it: *we are giving a prospect the opportunity to make an investment in the lives of our clients.*

When we ask people for money, we are trying to improve the quality of life of not only those we serve in our agencies, but also the quality of life of our donors.

In exchange for his or her money, the donor will have an impact on a human being who has far fewer resources. What greater gift is there than realizing that you have "added your light to the sum of light," and improved the quality of someone else's life?

3. *We should increase the number of individuals on our boards*

who have wealth and power. The place to start is with the nominating committee. In terms of fund raising, the chairperson of this committee should come to value these characteristics: a willingness and capacity to make a large gift early, a willingness and capacity to be visible and accessible to other board members, and, because of his or her wealth and status, the ability to manage the process of arranging cultivation contacts between other key leaders in the community and members of your staff and board.

4. *We should tell prospective board members before they accept the position that they are expected to make a financial gift to our agencies.* Period. If we are uncomfortable with a direct ask, find out what our colleagues are doing. Here are a couple of ideas that will make it less painful until you have developed a board culture where giving is a given:

a. Invite the prospect, face-to-face, to join the Board. Slide a form across the table and suggest that if he is interested, he needs to fill it out.

   The form should begin by asking for such items as a recent resume and a black and white studio photograph. Explain on the form that these will be useful for press releases. Ask for other general items of information, but include, at the bottom of the form, a section that says, roughly, "Please indicate at what level you intend to make your annual gift." Then do the little boxes with $25__ , $50__ , $100__ , Other__ or whatever.

b. If the best time to ask board members for money is early, the best person to do the asking is your board chairperson or president, although it can also be done by the chairperson of your development or nominating committees. An effective and reasonable approach is to suggest this:

   We understand that most of us have a number of charities that we support. However, we would hope, Bob, that during your tenure as a board member of Parmadale, you would make Parmadale one of your top two to three charities in terms of your annual gift.

The board member then makes his or her gift without a specific amount requested. Later, knowing what the baseline gift was, you can ask for a certain percentage increase.

5. *Establish that the ownership of your fund-raising programs must be shared.* To be successful, the responsibility and ownership of your efforts must be shared among the director, the board leadership, and, if you have one, your development director. If you don't insist on this level of teamwork, you'll find yourselves finger pointing and projecting the blame when you fail or are mutually disappointed on a project.[2]

6. *Strive for one hundred percent financial support from your board.* There are several reasons for this. One is that some foundations won't even consider making a grant without such a vote of confidence from board members. They figure, if those volunteer members in the community who are closest to your agency—your board—won't even support you, why should we? Another is that you will need to count on your board members to ask other people for money, and it's unlikely that they will ask others if they haven't made their own gift first. The last and most obvious reason is that this is an additional stream of income.

7. *Motivate and train board members to ask other people for money.* Give them training and literature if they want it. It will help those who truly seek it and will remove one or two more excuses from those who are actually too anxious to try.

8. *Remember that like anyone else, people with wealth and power feel more comfortable with peers, people they know, or people they have something in common with.* Getting that first person of influence on your board is the hardest. It gets easier as he or she begins to recruit colleagues and friends.

9. There's a good chance that you may not be extremely wealthy. Call me a psychic . . . I just have this feeling. However, I think it's very important that you remember (or discover) that *you still have social power and influence in your role as director*

of the agency. The reality of your role as steward of your agency will help to relieve the awkwardness you may feel when dealing with the rich and famous you're trying to seduce.

10. *If you make a bad decision and discover you have a weak board volunteer in a critical development leadership position, cut your losses and give him a mug.* This is not meant to be unkind. It's simply that given the scarcity of influential people on our boards and the urgent need for increased funding, we sometimes make the wrong decisions about our leadership. It's far better to wait for the right volunteer to successfully lead a campaign than to ask, in our impatience, someone who is presently available but not able to produce results.

11. *Give board members concrete, measurable, and attainable objectives.* Each board member should always know the answers to these three questions: what do you want me to do, when do you want me to do it by, and how will I know when I'm done whether I've been successful?

Haven't we all volunteered for something and seen a hundred other volunteers at the first meeting but then, months later, by the time the leadership got its act together to assign work, there were only, say, five people left?

12. An auxiliary board or council formed strictly to raise money should be considered only as a last resort and only if one hundred percent of the board members agree to lead the war by making their own sacrificial gifts. If an auxiliary is formed because of board members' reluctance to make personal gifts or ask others for money, don't expect much from the auxiliary.

On the other hand, if the auxiliary is formed with the intention to give board members more time to deal with the other business of guiding the agency, an auxiliary fund-raising group can be a tremendous asset to you.

13. Remember that you are not the only agency director reading this book or others like it. The top corporate leaders in all of our communities are the subject of small nonprofit breakfast schemes and the objective of huge college development

machines. *Knowing that most of these top people were mentored into their position, consider identifying and recruiting their pro-tégés.* If you are in it for the long term, an investment now in the number two or three person in an organization can pay huge dividends later. [3]

14. *If you are starting from scratch, your goal should be to go from a staff-driven fund-raising organizaion to a volunteer-driven organization.* If little or nothing is already in place, you will have no choice but to count on staff initiative to create an organization that can raise money successfully. The advantage is that you are more or less in control of the pace and the process. However, a staff-dominant fund-raising agency has at least two major disadvantages: a) you will be very tired most of the time, and, more important, b) you will limit the amount of money you can raise.

If you have been successful as a staff-driven agency, you will by definition be aggressive, bold, controlling, and superorganized. The trick then becomes how to pass the baton to your volunteers—i.e., how to relinquish some of that control, empower your volunteers, and take a supportive rather than a leadership role.

Nothing is impossible if you work together and pay less attention to who gets credit for what. You will be pleased to discover how much easier it is to get board members to ask other people for money *after* they have made their own gifts. Once you have people on your board who are capable of making their own gifts and are willing to, you may even start to have some fun applying the principles of the next chapter.

3 Developing a Major Gifts Program

Examples are few of men ruined by giving.
—Bovee

The phrase, "major donor prospect," just rolls off your tongue, doesn't it? The characteristics of people who earn this description are:

- wealthy—because they have discretionary income,
- interested in your cause, and
- philanthropic.

If you don't have all three ingredients, you probably don't have a "major donor prospect."

During the early years of Parmadale's fund-raising journey, we knew many people who were interested in us and were very charitable, but who didn't have much money. We also knew a few people who liked us and had a great deal of money, but weren't very philanthropic.[1]

We just didn't have all three ingredients working for us at the same time.

We concluded there had to be wealthy and philanthropic people out there somewhere who could learn to love us if given half a chance, kind of like the unmet stranger.

Embrace the following principles and take these action steps and you will soon begin to develop relationships with people who have all of these qualities. These steps, naturally, are simple but not easy.

Toward raising money from major donors

1. *Come to understand and accept the advantage of finding someone to make the solicitation who is difficult to say no to.* A critical component in major donor solicitation, the key to getting major gifts from individuals or corporations, is *who* does the asking. *Our job is to inspire someone to ask a major donor prospect for money, but that someone has to be someone who the prospect finds it difficult to say no to.*

Many of us have a great book on our desks titled, *The Fund Raisers' Guide to Private Fortunes.* It lists all Americans who have at least $10 million worth of identifiable assets and substantial participation in either the nonprofit or philanthropic sectors. [2]

Unfortunately, I could pick up the phone and ask every one of them for money and would bet my next paycheck that each of them would find it very easy to say no to me.

The key to making this resource work for us is thinking in terms of *relationship management.* Some larger universities actually have a staff whose only job is to move a board volunteer solicitor closer and closer to successful solicitation of a major donor prospect by keeping track of the prospect's interests and prompting the board volunteer in much the same way that a director would coach an actor.

There's an old poker adage that goes, "If you don't know who the pigeon is 20 minutes after you sit down at the table, it's you." Study your volunteers and prospects with at least the same level of thoughtfulness you would use to decide whether to hold your cards or fold them.

2. *Identify people who are wealthy (have disposable income) and who are philanthropic.* Call a meeting with your top staff and volunteers. The point of the meeting is to list the names of people who the group thinks fit this description. However, before you rush to your storeroom for flip charts, newsprint, chalk, and clean erasers, let me suggest one rule for the meeting:

> People around the table cannot offer the name of a person who they would not feel comfortable asking *themselves*.

There is one exception to this rule: it's all right if the nominator knows who would be a *better* candidate to ask and is willing to try to involve this person.

Without this rule, the group will spend two hours over lunch dropping all of the powerful and wealthy names they can think of and walk away feeling they accomplished something. At the next meeting, one or two new people will show up and suggest that you get somebody else to join the group and, next meeting, these new people show up and suggest you get somebody else to come to the meeting . . . ad infinitum.

If you allow this, and you promote what you permit, after six months, you'll have a steering committee of 90 people, five of whom are still coming to meetings, a food bill close to the cost of a small wedding, and a list of a few hundred members of your community who appear wealthy and who, if you called them and asked them for money, would say no.

You can put this list next to your copy of *Private Fortunes* on your coffee table.

3. *Try to involve competent accountants, investment brokers, trust officers or financial planners in the wealth assessment process.* They can help you determine whether a prospect really is capable of making a large gift. A friend in development told me how excited he was by a man who bought two tables to his

agency's formal dinner dance, owned his own company, had a beautiful home, and received some services from the agency about eight years earlier. He appeared to have all the characteristics of a major donor prospect. However, an investment banker volunteer pointed out that he could be mortgaged to the hilt, have kids ready to enter college, and may have purchased the tables through his corporation (which might not even be doing very well).

4. *Identify the volunteers from your team of board members who are the best possible people to make the solicitation.* If you conducted your prospect identification meetings well, this should be self-evident. However, since the number of major donor prospects you are targeting is small, it is wise to review each prospect with your committee to identify all possible links with other people who might know the prospect and be willing to help.

5. *Train and support board volunteers who will ultimately do the asking.* Assuming they want training, and most will if for no other reason than to buy time before actually having to ask someone else for money, you can provide it yourself by sharing articles, training guides, or books (see Suggested Reading). You can enroll the volunteer in workshops sponsored by local chapters of professional fund-raising organizations if they exist.

However, the simplest and, I think, most effective approach is hiring a moonlighting development person who has had experience with direct asking by board members or other volunteers. Check with your local colleges or cultural organizations. This can be a one-time presentation with reasonable phone follow-up and you can work out an affordable fee that is comfortable for both you and the consultant.

6. *Involve the major donor prospect with your agency.* This is a critical point. Here are some ways you can introduce prospects to your agency and begin to develop relationships.

    a. Invite them to a social function as guests of the board solicitor.

b. Invite them to a meal with you and the board contact. Let them understand beforehand that they will not be solicited for money.

c. Invite them to serve on a special event or public relations committee. These are nonconfrontational committees— i.e., a special event "ask" will involve a clear exchange, and no pitch, to speak of, is involved in public relations.

d. Invite them to serve on an auxiliary or advisory committee.

e. Invite them to serve on your board.

f. Simply ask them for their help. People are funny. Most of us feel closer to those we help (even those who may be annoyed at being asked in the first place).

7. *Where we tend to fail is in the longer-term follow-ups with prospects.* We bring them out for an event, pique their interest, send them home with an armful of materials, and don't see them again for nine months if ever.

Cultivate good relationships.

Create a rhythm in your agency where you regularly review a manageable number of your top volunteers and come up with ways to further develop these relationships. By rhythm, I mean that unless you set aside regular time to think about them, they will drift to the back of the stove and dry up.

Listen for cues. In 1984, a foundation director mentioned how much he liked the book, *1984*, by George Orwell. Within a few days after the meeting, we lent him a tape of the movie. Think of yourself as a salesman cultivating a relationship with a special client. If she likes baseball, take her to a game. If he likes theater, give him tickets.

8. *Have the right person make the right pitch at the right time for the right amount of money.* This is more art than science and timing really is everything. Give your volunteer a long leash in regard to when the solicitation is made, but do keep him on a leash. Remember that the natural entropy of volunteers, especially volunteers new to asking, will be to avoid making the call. After evaluating the prospect's capacity and willingness to make

a gift, ask down. Start with the largest amount reasonable and, if the answer is no, lower the request.

9. *Thank and recognize the donor in proportion to the gift.* When recognizing gifts, be sensitive to the donor's values, motivation, and temperament. Some people don't want attention. Others crave it. A friend received $15,000 from an individual early in his first capital campaign several years ago. He was ecstatic. In fact, he was so ecstatic it didn't even occur to him to thank him for nearly ten days after receiving the check. It just escaped him. Any future gifts from the guy has escaped him, too.

10. *Thank and support your solicitor.* Don't forget to thank your solicitor, but know that he or she will already be feeling great about the successful solicitation. Your solicitor will learn that no one complains about making a gift *after* it has been made. Philanthropy is a classic win–win activity.

*   *   *

If getting large gifts from a few people requires finesse and balance, getting small gifts from many people requires muscle and work.

4 Developing an Annual Fund

If you pursue evil with pleasure,
the pleasure passes and the evil remains.
If you pursue good with labor,
the labor passes and the good remains.

—Cicero

Foundations won't give you ongoing operations money. Government resources are lean. Where do you get money for development costs, public relations, new program development, special materials or equipment? Your annual fund.

The notion of an annual fund is unfamiliar to some of us. It is a term usually associated with colleges, private secondary schools, or cultural organizations.

More and more social service agencies, however, are coming to see the value of an annual fund as the primary source of donors who are interested in becoming involved with our agencies for a small price, but who may grow into major benefactors later.

Imagine a pyramid and the goal of raising a million dollars. One way to accomplish this, at the bottom of the pyramid, would be to ask a million people for a dollar each.

Another way is to ask one person for a million dollars.

This chapter suggests how to ask a million people for a dollar or, how you can develop an annual fund that will increase your donor base, create a pool of hot prospects from which larger gifts will come later, and raise unrestricted, nondesignated money.

Acquisition mailings

1. *Begin a program of acquisition mailings to prospects from rented, targeted lists.* With any kind of luck, this process will roughly be a financial wash in the beginning. However, due to increased mailing costs, more competition and a saturation of the marketplace, it is more difficult today to acquire new donors through direct mail and also break even.

Even though you won't raise any money in the early stages, you will begin to build your donor base.

One of the important points to remember about an increased donor base is that in addition to increased income from future solicitations, you'll also increase the pool of philanthropic people interested in your agency or cause who may become prospects for major gifts later.

If you attend to two important points in this process, the rest is only a matter of patience, information management, following directions and arithmetic. It's a no-brainer as long as you do the following:

   a. Clearly explain to your board that you will not raise money on this project in the first year or so. The hidden danger is that board members will approve the concept and then, five or six months later, will look at the numbers and forget the original intention—i.e., to increase your donor base, a base that will begin to be very profitable in your second and subsequent years. Otherwise, they might say, "let's not do THAT again, we didn't make any money on it."
   b. Write a creative single-page letter. As competition continues to increase, it will become even more important that

your single-page letter captures the reader quickly and moves him to a gift. A longer letter can, of course, be very effective when appealing to established donors. However, you will keep your costs down in your acquisition mailings if you can make your case in a one-pager.

Assuming board support, a creative letter, and a well-targeted rental list, the acquisition mailing becomes strictly a matter of mathematics and work. If you mail 10,000 solicitation letters to people on a list rented from a broker, you'll get about a .015 percent response, or 150 donors. If their average gift is, say, $30, you will gross $4,500. It may cost you close to this or more, though, to do the mailing.

However, six months from now, when you return to these new donors with your next letter (at a very low cost, of course), you can expect between 30 and 50% of them to make a gift. The math here is 50% of 150 donors = 75 donors. Seventy-five donors × $30 average gift = $2,250. This time you have netted nearly $2,250. Then you repeat the process.

This process is not expensive, but it is very labor-intensive. *And, remember, if you do not follow through with your new donors, it will be a waste of time, energy and money.*

2. *Send a thank you to all donors within 48 hours after receiving the gift.* You can do these by using a computer and a good letter-quality printer. It's much more powerful and personal, though, if you handwrite a short note of thanks. Consider a compromise: do personalized form letters with a hand-written postscript.

3. *Continue your acquisition program by mailing appeal letters to logical prospects such as friends and families of staff and volunteers, local merchants, local residents, etc.*

4. The bad news is that more organizations will be sending direct mail to wider audiences. The good news is that *segmentation and computer technology will help us mail only to prospects who are likely to respond* (or, at least, more likely to respond than others). Use a rifle rather than a shotgun approach.

5. *Those who have a strong public awareness and good name recognition in the community will grow more rapidly.* This suggests the need to improve our public relations activities.

Upgraded donor mailings

1. Take steps to *upgrade gifts from present donors.* Assuming that you haven't already conducted an upgrade campaign, you can expect some very good results.

There are a number of ways to do this, but they, too, are labor-intensive and in this case would involve both staff *and* volunteer time. Techniques include creating gift clubs, recognition programs, a volunteer-driven pyramid campaign featuring personal solicitations, phone-call or gift-pickup follow-ups, second mailings, etc.

2. *Write creative, emotional letters.* I know this sounds like, "first buy a high-rise apartment," but it is very important. If you don't have any right-brain verbal artists on your staff, look for volunteer help. As a rule, people who give to human and social service agencies are not motivated by a sense of indebtedness, such as college alumni, and they are not expecting a social perk such as patrons of cultural organizations. They are more likely to be motivated by a general sense or awareness of pain and need in the world. Social justice issues are important to them.

A direct mail solicitation gives people the opportunity to make a small difference with the hope that if enough people do likewise, their gift will result in an improved quality of life for someone somewhere.

Therefore, *your one-page solicitation letter should be a powerful emotional appeal to these values.* This isn't to say that your letter should be a tear jerker in the spirit of a movie-of-the-week melodrama. It is to say that you're likely to get better results by provoking strong *feelings* as well as thoughts. A theologian once said, "I set myself on fire and people come to watch me burn." The flame from a creative letter will attract people to you.

3. *You will increase your response to direct mail letters by following up with a phone call.* This is inexpensive and hard work. Your phone follow-up can be as simple as asking a half-dozen volunteers to spend a day making phone calls or as sophisticated as having 50 volunteers in a four-week, competitive phone campaign where volunteers are paid for their successes.

The point is that you will increase your income by the extra personal contact after the letter.

Here are a few comments and rules of thumb for phone drives:

a. Be selective in choosing your volunteers. You don't want to annoy your prospects with callers who are grating, surly, overly aggressive, or apt to react poorly to criticism or a negative response by a prospect.

b. If your agency can't support a phone drive, you can generally find a corporation that will lend you its offices after business hours to make phone calls.

c. Paid volunteers sometimes do better than unpaid volunteers.

d. Younger volunteers usually become less upset with negative responses. Articulate college-age callers are good choices because they'll continue making calls after being rejected while the same rejection is likely to drive an older caller into a reflective (and nonproductive) existential crisis.

4. *Gimmick mail will decrease; more personalized-looking mail will increase.* Stamps should be put on letters rather than meter imprints. I personally never open third-class mail unless it has a great envelope "hook" and I want to see the technique used.

5. *Building and cultivating a relationship with donors will be critical to keeping them.* There's too much competition. Look for ways to get donors involved.

6. *Create gift clubs.* Call them whatever you want and make gift ranges of $500, $1,000, $2,500, and $5,000. Start by offering minimum recognition for your first level—e.g., a membership card and copy of the newsletter. The second level could include the card, the newsletter, a mug with your agency name on it,

and an invitation to an open house. The third level could include all of these in addition to a lapel pin or pen. The top level could include all the preceding and an invitation to a dinner at the home of the president of your board.

7. Increase your income by segmenting your donors by the size of their gifts. *Raise the small gifts a higher percentage than larger gifts.* For example, people in the $25 gift range could go to $35. Someone giving $1,000 could go to $1,250. You should shoot for between 60 and 75% *renewal rate* from donors.

Prospect research

There are several steps you can take toward developing a donor base.

1. The first is to jump-start your base by *developing a list of the inner circles of your board, staff, and other volunteers.* At Parmadale, we started with staff, family members, and friends and just killed each other with solicitations. After a year of this my own mother wouldn't return my phone calls. Today, we don't solicit staff for anything. We invite them if they are interested, but there is no pressure.

After your friends and family, identify ever-expanding concentric circles of contracts—e.g., neighbors, local merchants, suppliers and vendors, local government officials, etc. Next, identify people in the general community who might have a natural interest in your cause—e.g., doctors and nurses if you provide social service aftercare to burn victims or donors to a large national children's organization if you provide local children's services, foundations, civic groups, etc. Finally, approach the general public, beginning with those who are physically closest to you.

Write up a profile of all the characteristics of the type of person who would be likely to support your organization. The first place to look, for example, would be natural benefactors, people who have been served directly. The problem here, of course, is that those of us whose clients are the disadvantaged, the needy, can't turn to these same clients for financial help.

2. *Go to a good list broker with your profile and rent lists.* For example, we asked for a list of names of Catholic females, 55 years old or older, who had a record of giving to human service organizations.

Look for characteristics such as age (people in the 35–64 age range are generally good donors, although the best are 50–64 years old), past giving patterns if your broker has this information, geographical locations, gender, religion, marital status, etc.

The face-to-face membership drive

1. *Conduct one membership drive every year.* If you don't already have something people can be a member of, make something up. Create a "Friends of Tuna Society" or some such thing. People love to get a membership card even though it may mean absolutely nothing. I was a "loyal member" of AAA for seven years and let my membership expire. When I renewed, I got a new card and the little circle in the right hand corner said that I was a "loyal member" for only one year. I was sick about it.

2. A modest example of how to sell memberships in your friends group or society through a pyramid approach is:

a. Ask a key volunteer to lead your four-week membership campaign and get five people (friends, relatives, colleagues, etc.) to be captains. Each of these friends will be expected to get five of their own friends. That should make 31 people. Ask each of them to sell five memberships for $35 apiece. Here's the math: 31 people × $35 cost of membership × 5 memberships each = $5,425.

b. Hold a kickoff brunch and a victory dinner at the end. Have a report meeting somewhere between the start and close. You'll net a few thousand dollars and, if your volunteers enjoy it, you can raise tens of thousands of dollars a year to add to your annual fund.

You can have as large a volunteer organization as you wish, and increase funds raised proportionately, but the larger the organization, the more demanding your management tasks will be.

3. The steps of a *typical face-to-face membership drive* are:
   a. Set your campaign goals.
   b. Develop campaign publicity and promotional materials.
   c. Identify and rate prospects.
   d. Recruit volunteers.
   e. Orient volunteers.
   f. Assign prospects to volunteers.
   g. Meet with volunteers throughout the campaign.
   h. Kick off the campaign and begin soliciting prospects.
   i. Conduct volunteer progress report meetings.
   j. Acknowledge gifts within 48 hours if possible.
   k. Keep good records.
   l. Prepare final reports.
   m. Reward or recognize volunteers and donors.
   n. Evaluate and set goals for next year.

Developing your volunteer network

1. Direct mail solicitations, phone calls, and membership drives are areas where *nonboard volunteers* can be a major asset. The key is to be organized. Be prepared to keep volunteers busy with such activities as:
   a. Recording information—e.g., input from phone calls, gift data entry into computer, or cards following the reception of a gift in the mail;
   b. Collating, addressing, stuffing, licking, stamping, bagging, and mailing;
   c. Teaching, overseeing, and motivating other volunteers;
   d. Recruiting other volunteers.

2. We must *be ready to spend a lot of time with our volunteers*, even after the initial investment of orientation and training has been accomplished. Volunteers who contribute time working on

details can be supervised by other staff; but those asking for money and representing your agency need your own time or that of your top staff.

3. *Volunteers need to be challenged.* However, we shouldn't set goals for them that they cannot attain. Volunteers have a lower tolerance for failure than staff. They also are less motivated to risk future failure by continuing to work in the system that may have set them up for failure in the first place by giving them unrealistic goals.

4. The delicate balance in working with volunteers is this: on one hand, we need to be aggressive enough with them, demanding enough, that they *work* between meetings, yet, on the other hand, not so demanding that we alienate them and lose them.

5. Another challenge in working with volunteers lies in *defining their boundaries.* They need enough freedom to make some independent decisions about the course of their work, yet not so much that they lose sight of their goals and objectives.

6. Volunteers will do well if they are given simple and singular assignments, have high visibility, are not required to attend too many meetings, their work does not extend too long over a period—e.g., 18–24 months—and you recognize their work publicly.[1]

*   *   *

If you've never asked for money by mail or phone before, or if you haven't asked for a long time or for much, expect that someone is going to say something like, "It seems that every time you turn around, they've got their hand in your pocket again." Don't let this throw you off your plan. Organizations that have been successfully fund raising for years often mail between eight and twelve times a year to donors.

5 The Zen of Grantsmanship

Writing is easy. All you do is stare at a blank sheet of paper until drops of blood form on your forehead.

—Gene Fowler

Style

Over the years, my wife, Anne, has frequently asked me to help her reword something she has written. The formula is always the same. Before I respond she adds, "What I meant to say was . . ." and then proceeds to tell me what she meant to say. I write this down, usually word for word. She says thanks and walks away thinking I'm a great writer.

When Anne talks she is unconscious of her techniques. She mastered grammar (like most of us) by the time she was in the first grade. She got a handle on usage by the time she graduated from high school. In conversation, she articulates her thoughts beautifully. When she talks, she talks effortlessly, thinking only about her message and her listener. She has mastered the Zen of conversation.

Zen has to do with the state we achieve when, through

repetition and the application of a variety of disciplines, we perform a behavior effortlessly. I like to think that it's the state we reach when we do things without being conscious of our techniques while being totally conscious of the present moment. An important ingredient in Zen is *getting ourselves out of the way* and I think that this is a state or quality we should strive for when writing grant proposals.

We can all approach this Zen state in grant writing if we learn and practice the basics. The suggestions that follow are offered to remind you of some principles you may already know but have forgotten and to teach you some new ones to improve your grant writing skills.

1. *Practice the Zen of grant writing.* We need to get ourselves out of the way when we write grants. I don't let myself become self-conscious when I write. When I speak to groups, if I'm thinking mostly about myself instead of mostly about my message and you, I do a mediocre job at best and flake out at worst. I write best when I am focused on sharing my message by putting myself in the reader's place. If I am constantly "adjusting my tie," so to speak, asking myself, "how do I look?" in my writing, I don't write very well at all. This state gets easier after you've learned and practiced the basics.

Improve your skills by learning the techniques and then practicing them. Go to workshops, read books and articles, talk to others, find a mentor. But, most important, just do it. Like anything, given proper instruction, you will get better and better with practice. If you are having a problem with your writing, walk away from it and ask yourself aloud, "What did I mean to say here?" Then, write down your answer to that question.

2. *Write proposals to Aunt Sylvia.* When I write grants, I write them so my Aunt Sylvia can understand them. Don't write to a faceless committee; write to someone you know. This will personalize your grants and make them more readable. E. B. White said, "Don't write about Man, write about a man."

3. *Don't bind the proposals unless the foundation asks for*

multiple copies. If they ask for only one or two copies, use paper clips because the first thing they will do is to rip it apart and make their own copies.

4. *Pay attention to mechanics and logistics.* Make sure that you follow the guidelines given to you by foundations. Send them the right number of copies. Make sure the proper signatures appear on your proposal. Make sure you have proper postage. Address the proposal to the right person. Double-space your proposal. Use wide margins all around. Do not use a justified right margin even if you have it on your computer. It isn't as readable as ragged right. Don't miss any small detail that will give the foundation a reason to screen you out of competition before staff members even read your grant request.

5. *Revise.* Sidney Smith said, "In composing, as a general rule, run a pen through every other word that you have written; you have no idea what rigor it will give your style." Carve fat. Mark Twain said, "Forgive me for writing such a long letter. I didn't have time to write a short one." Gustave Flaubert said, "Whenever you can shorten a sentence, do. And one always can. The best sentence? The shortest." Brevity takes time, but you'll give your writing muscle if you make the effort.

6. *Never stop writing when you don't know what to say next.* Stop when you know *exactly* what you're going to say next. This reduces our tendency to avoid returning to a writing project. (A corollary of this is to stop reading when your book is interesting, not when it is dull.)

7. *End your paragraphs with power.* Put your power words at the end of sentences and paragraphs. Put your power paragraphs at the end of sections. For example,

Arnold's mother was responsible for his broken leg, according to the 1990 Child Advocacy Report.

According to the 1990 Child Advocacy Report, Arnold's mother was responsible for his broken leg.

8. *Use creative detail.* There is a place for data in a proposal and there is a place for pictures. When you want to create an image in the reader's mind, use visual detail. See how the following image is sharpened by adding only five words of detail:

> Caesar's body was carried out of the forum on a stretcher.
> Caesar's body was carried out of the forum on a stretcher, his left arm hanging down.

9. *Don't inflate your language.* If I let myself imagine that I'm writing to that group of industrialists under the bar graphs, I will tend to inflate my language. Jack Woodford said, "One of your first jobs, as you write for money, will be to get rid of your vocabulary." Don't be pompous.

10. *Rewrite anything written by a committee.* Even if some of the committee members have great style and good content, rewrite everything in your own voice so it is unified.

11. *Be original and fresh in your writing style, but don't get too clever.* I recently wrote a sentence in a proposal that described our agency as being "fat-free." The context was that Parmadale is a well-managed, efficiently operated agency that uses its financial resources wisely. After rereading the proposal, I decided that the sentence would interrupt the reader's flow or draw attention to itself. I revised it and said that our organization is lean and efficient.

12. *Blank paper is hypnotic.* If you are stuck, jump-start your grant writing by putting anything at all on the paper. Write a letter to yourself about the grant. Write down key ideas. Write a poem. Anything. You can always revise later. Sometimes, if I'm stuck getting started, I'll start **anywhere**—at the end or in the middle. Just write.

13. *Choose your style thoughtfully.* Many veteran grant writers insist on always writing in the third person to create distance between the writer and the content. However, I had an experience writing a research proposal that I began as academically as

possible and was advised by a foundation liaison that the review board "hates dusty, dry proposals." My revised version contained numerous anecdotes and human interest stories. I wrote in the first person plural—i.e., we—and we received a two-year award.

On the other hand, a large local foundation has indicated that they prefer to read proposals written in the third person.

Know your audience and choose a style that will have the most impact.

14. *Make sure you ask for money.* I always ask for money twice, once in the cover letter and again in the summary statement. I usually say, "Parmadale respectfully requests a grant of $50,000 to . . ."

15. *After you've written the proposal, give it to someone completely unfamiliar with the work you do to see if it makes sense.* Your foundation reviewer is likely to have the same perspective as your friend or relative.

I've played golf for 28 years. Last summer, desperate to improve my game, I went to a golf instructor. I told him I have spent nearly as much time practicing on driving ranges as I have playing on golf courses. He said that all my years of practice have made me very good at playing badly. His point was that practice, or repetition, is not enough. I need to practice the proper techniques, repeat the right moves, over and over before I will improve.

To improve your grant writing skills, practice alone is not enough. Learn good techniques and practice them when you write grants. In time, you'll find yourself much less self-conscious, be able to think more freely and creatively about your subject, and, ultimately, raise much more money for your agency.

Research

1. *Use the resources of the Foundation Center.* The Foundation Center has its main office in New York City; its national collec-

tions are in both Washington, D.C., and New York. These collections contain information on virtually all of the foundations in the country. Its field offices in Cleveland and San Francisco provide the same information as the national collections with the exception of tax returns, which are only regional.

The Foundation Center maintains a series of cooperating collections in more than 170 cities throughout the country in public and university libraries. To learn what collection is closest to you, call 1-800-424-9836.

2. *Do your homework.* Many agencies don't do proper research and, as a result, submit to inappropriate, untargeted foundations and get rejected quickly. This tends to reinforce whatever apprehensions the grant seeker might have had in the first place. Research foundations before submitting proposals.[1]

Foundations are annoyed (to put it mildly) by agencies that submit proposals without bothering to determine whether the submission is appropriate. Don't use a shotgun approach: use a rifle.

Trained volunteers can be very helpful in doing foundation research. At Parmadale, a team of 12 volunteers discovered 321 foundations for our capital campaign from the *Foundation Directory* at the Foundation Center Library. Phone calls to each reduced the group to 101. We submitted proposals to all of them over a ten-week period and received gifts from 28 for a total of $380,000.

3. An excellent resource for grant seeking social and human service agencies is the annual *Fund Raiser's Guide to Human Service Funding*, published by The Taft Group. It is indexed by headquarters, geographic preference, grant type and recipient type and includes targets such as the aged, drugs and alcohol, employment, youth services, family services, and crime.

4. You will find, with few exceptions, that *it will be difficult to get ongoing funding for operations.* This sad reality strengthens

the case for developing your annual fund, your best source for undesignated, unrestricted funding.

Relationships

1. *Most small foundations are unstaffed.* Relationships have more of an influence on how your proposal is reviewed with a small foundation. It helps if the grant reviewers can connect a face with the proposal they are reviewing. A director of a local foundation said that an agency increases its chances of getting funded "by up to seventy-five percent" if a personal contact has been made. After you have done your research and targeted a foundation for submission, make a phone call for current information. Try to get a representative to visit your agency. If that effort is unsuccessful, try to get a 20-minute face-to-face visit at the foundation office. If you get it, be prepared to leave after 20 minutes.

There are two qualifications to this rule of thumb:

   a. A proposal should be able to stand alone. It should be fundable based on a strongly written case that matches an allocation priority of the foundation. Some foundations discourage face-to-face contact because of the incredible volume of grant seekers.

   b. Be cautious when trying to influence a foundation reviewer. You may self-destruct by going over the head of a program officer whose job it is to do a first review of your proposal and make a recommendation to the review committee.

2. *However, larger staffed foundations will be less apt to be influenced by relationships.* The merit of your proposal will drive the decision of larger foundations to a much greater extent than good relationships or "who you know."

3. *Do not think of the relationship between the foundation and you as adversarial.* Think of the relationship as a potential partnership. It can't do its job without us and we can't do our job

without it. In fact, **we** do all the work and the foundation knows and appreciates this.

4. *Once a foundation decides to fund your project, it will become one of your greatest advocates to others, including other foundations.* Make sure to follow through promptly and professionally with all required foundation reports and evaluations. In other words, work as hard to maintain your relationship *after* you receive the grant as you did to get it.

5. *Don't let rejections get you down.* Get as much constructive feedback as you can from every rejection and then press on. If criticism is valid, make corrections and move on. Forget about dropping the ball in yesterday's game.

Ask the foundation why you were turned down. If it says that it liked your idea but had insufficient funds, ask if you could resubmit your proposal in the next funding cycle. If the foundation identifies a weakness in your case, ask for help to fix it. Then do so and resubmit. If the foundation says it wasn't a priority, you probably should have known this and not submitted it in the first place. Persist.

Besides trying to get your proposal funded, this is an excellent opportunity to develop a personal relationship with the foundation and affirm your credibility.

6. If you are in a location where foundation representatives do public presentations describing their allocation interests, funding guidelines, etc., *take these opportunities to introduce yourself to them.* I like to arrive at these meetings very early, knowing that the presenters often will arrive early, too, to get a feel for the room and setup. You have a better chance of being remembered with this kind of introduction than if you are a member of the stampede trying to make contact afterwards with a very tired presenter who is looking forward to going home.

7. *Get as much local PR as possible.* Most social service agencies have good reputations, but low profiles. Agencies that have been around for many years can establish credibility fairly

easily in their proposals. Agencies without a long and successful history need to begin to build an image in the community.

Structure

The following structure for developing a grant proposal draws heavily upon *Program Planning and Proposal Writing* by Norton J. Kiritz, President of the Grantsmanship Center located at 1125 West Sixth Street, Fifth Floor, P.O. Box 17220, Los Angeles, California 90017. This organization also provides very good workshop experiences.[2]

The following structure for a proposal is useful not only for foundation proposals, but even for government or corporate grants. However, if a particular foundation provides its own guidelines and they are different from the following, *use the foundation's own guidelines.*

The cover letter

Proposals are usually accompanied by a cover letter with an authorizing signature. Have the director cosign it with the chairperson of your board.

The cover letter should briefly describe the content of the proposal. This letter also gives you the opportunity to suggest a follow-up—e.g., "We would welcome the opportunity to meet with you . . ." or "Please contact us at . . ."

Don't be presumptuous in your tone. That is, don't tell the readers that they should fund your proposal. For example, don't say things like, "We know that you will find this proposal to be of great significance," or "Surely it is obvious to you that . . ."

On the other hand, don't beg. Foundations are in the business of giving money away.

And, finally, don't try to make a case that if you don't get funded your agency or organization is sunk. People like to invest money in organizations that are moving in the right direction rather than in ones that are characterized as camping on the brink of disaster.

Title page

I put a title about 20 lines down the page. An inch or two below that I indicate to whom I am sending the grant. At the bottom, centered, I put our agency name, address, and phone along with the names of the director, and board chairpersons and my own name as contact person. Finally, I put the date.

Table of contents

Self-explanatory.

Executive summary

The rule is to write this last and put it first. It should never be more than one page. Single-space it if you absolutely have to.

Introduction

Agencies that have a high profile in the community, long-term good reputation, or a previous relationship with the funder can minimize the length of this section. If, however, your agency is new, low-profile, or has had some negative publicity in the last few years, make a statement in this section that improves your credibility.

Needs assessment

This is the most critical piece of your proposal. It is also the most commonly under-developed or poorly developed.

1. The first and most important point to remember when writing a needs assessment is to *describe the problem in relation-*

ship to the community rather than in relationship to your agency. Foundations aren't interested in your agency's problems. They are interested in solving problems and meeting needs in the community. Foundations aren't interested in the leaking pipes in the basement of your home for retarded adolescents. But they could become interested if fixing these pipes would mean improving services to these same kids.

2. *Ask yourself, "How hard do I have to work to make my case?"* Parmadale provides homes for nearly 200 young people who have serious problems. Several years ago, when we had no way to air condition the homes, I approached a foundation. The program officer was sympathetic, but said that we were going to have to work real hard to make our case since it was competing with such needs as hunger, shelter, and jobs.

3. *Weak problem statements usually begin with a general idea that something is wrong.* For example, general ideas would be stated something like this:[3]

Our schools are deteriorating.
This country has a welfare problem
Teenage pregnancy is reaching epidemic proportions.
Racism exists in public schools.

Many of us have a tendency to stop the assessment process at this point. Having stated the problem or needs broadly, we want to rush into action and seek solutions without giving enough forethought or analysis to developing our problem statement more precisely.

4. We tend to express needs or problems in *vague* or *ambiguous* terms.

Vague terms have too little meaning. Ambiguous terms have multiple meanings. "This country has a welfare problem" could mean that too many people are ripping off the system or it could imply that too many needy people are going without food or places to live.

5. *Here are the steps to take to write a good problem statement.*

Step One

Begin to write your statement by answering these questions:
a. Where does the problem exist?
b. Who, specifically, is affected by it?
c. When does it occur?
d. To what degree or extent is it felt?

Step Two

Add the phrase "as evidenced by" to your problem statement.

Step Three

List as many *contributing factors* to the problem as you can think of. For example, a contributing factor influencing the behavior of sex-offending adolescents is the fact that they were sexually abused themselves. The cycle of abuse continues.

Step Four

List the specific *consequences* of the problem if the problem goes unsolved or the need unmet.

In the example of sex-offending adolescents, a kid who goes untreated is likely to offend 300 more times in his or her lifetime, involving 40 victims or more.

Step Five

Select which of the contributing factors to the problem you will address and which you wish to postpone. In other words, select priorities.

Determine what aspects of the problem, what contributing factors, are most important and you are most likely to solve. Try to narrow the problem down to parts that you can be reasonably certain you can successfully solve. You want to choose the parts of the problem that have *realistic* and *attainable* solutions.

To do this you should examine your list of contributing factors while asking yourself these questions:
a. What are we able or capable of doing something about?

b. What do we choose or elect to do something about?

Rewrite your problem statement to include these changes. Polish it. You should now have written a fairly exhaustive description of your problem.

Objectives

Now that the community's needs are selected and defined, it is possible to set objectives that are statements of what you intend to accomplish, of what needs, specifically, you intend to meet.

1. Your yardstick for success will become the extent to which you accomplish your objectives. By setting objectives that are specifically related to your problem statement, you can later tell whether you were fully or partially successful in resolving the problem.

2. Your objectives should describe the outcome of your proposal in measurable terms.

3. At least one *objective should be matched to each problem or need* described in your problem statement.

4. Objectives should reflect *change*. You should be able to measure the degree of change you effect. For example, we might say, as a problem, that 100 children read at two grade levels below average. An objective might be to increase seventy-five percent of these kids' reading grade levels by two years during one year of education in your special reading program.

5. Objectives should be *relevant*. They will be relevant if they address the problem as stated. Your problem statement expresses a situation in negative terms. Something is wrong. An objective states a desirable situation to be achieved. It is intended to correct the problem.

6. Objectives should be *attainable and realistic*. They should be capable of being realized. Your problem statement may reflect a larger condition than can be corrected by an objective. This often means that the entire problem will not be eliminated.

7. Objectives should be *measurable* because they are based on tangible, concrete, and quantifiable results.

Methods

Methods describe the activities to be conducted to achieve your desired objectives. It is the how-to or cookbook section of your proposal.

Describe your program activities in this section. Clearly state your reasons for selecting these activities. Describe the chronological sequence of activities in an outline format. Describe your staffing patterns in terms of qualifications, functions, time needed, etc.

In short, describe any practical and logical activities that have to do with the actual techniques you will use to deliver your services in order to meet your objectives.

Budget

Your budget should describe your costs.

    a. Your budget should be sufficient to perform the tasks described in your narrative.

    b. Your budget should detail all personnel and nonpersonnel costs.

    c. Your budget should contain no unexplained items for miscellaneous needs or contingencies.

Don't pad your budget as some grant seekers do. However, many social and human service agencies, apprehensive to start with, tend not to ask for enough.

A project might actually cost $100,000, but, afraid of failing, the agency asks for only $75,000. The foundation then asks if it can conduct the project if the agency only receive $50,000 and the agency says it can! Request what you need to do the job. Foundations have a good sense of what is needed to run programs and provide services.

Evaluation

This piece presents a plan for determining the extent to which your objectives are met. You should strive to include these ingredients in your evaluation:

a. Present a plan for evaluating the achievement of your objectives.
b. Present a plan for modifying methods on an ongoing basis over the course of your program.
c. Tell who will be doing the evaluation and how they were chosen.
d. Explain any test instruments or questionnaires to be used.
e. Describe any evaluation reports to be produced—e.g., quarterly, semiannually, final, etc.

Future funding

This section should describe your plan for continuing funding, if necessary, beyond the time of your grant funding.

a. Present a specific plan to obtain future funding if your program is to be continued.
b. Describe how other funds will be obtained if necessary to supplement the grant.
c. Present letters of commitment if possible.

Appendix

This section should contain copies of the following:

a. Your 501(c)3 number (which establishes your classification as a nonprofit, tax-exempt organization)
b. Your most recent audited financial statement
c. Names of board members
d. Letters of support from authorities, key people

e. Added documentation that supports materials in the body of your proposal
f. Illustrative materials—e.g., good flier, brochure

6 Corporate Philanthropy: An Oxymoron?

The underlying philosophy of corporate philanthropy is that it is good business to be an enlightened corporate citizen. It doesn't make sense to talk about successful corporations in a society whose schools, hospitals, churches, symphonies, or libraries are deteriorating or closing."

—Clifton C. Garvin, Jr.

Corporations were not the first potential funding source to occur to human service agency directors in the 1960s or 1970s. In fact, they were usually the last.

Following the combination of reductions of government funding and increases in private and community foundation solicitations, we seemed to "discover" the corporate community as an untapped source. With the exception of a relatively small number of innovative partnerships formed by aggressive and creative agencies, this source has proven to be less accessible than its early reviews would have indicated.

However, in spite of the difficulties in getting their support, corporations remain a resource. Here are some guidelines and suggestions:

1. *Corporations, unlike foundations, are not in the business of*

giving money away. Corporations that are accountable to their stockholders are unlikely to give money away without being able to demonstrate a return on their investment. If your programs and services do not make some kind of quid pro quo sense to a corporation, you won't get funded.

2. *Corporations, like foundations, want to see quantifiable results.* Businesses are bottom-line-oriented. They express their results in numbers. You'll increase your potential for funding if you are able to demonstrate the extent to which their gift will make an impact on a common problem or need.

3. *In general, corporations tend to be interested in projects that have an impact on local neighborhoods, education, health, the arts, and civic affairs.* Those that do feel an obligation to help social or human service causes often meet it through gifts to United Way Services.

4. *If you receive United Way Services funds, you are aware of the constraints in place to ensure that agencies do not double-solicit corporations.* These constraints usually involve the timing of special events, restrictions on mass acquisition mailings, and eligibility for corporate matching gifts programs. However, I suggest that you strive to form partnerships with your local United Way that will be mutually beneficial. For example, many United Way organizations have leadership development programs that provide interested agencies with a pool of interested, mid- to upper-management-level business people who would make good board candidates or serve as volunteers.

5. *Know the economic landscape.* Research corporations you intend to approach the same way you research foundations. Look for the relevance of your agency's mission to the corporation's community interests. Know the corporate players and what they are interested in. Shotgun submissions irritate corporations.

6. *Whether or not you believe, politically, that social and human service agencies are "entitled" to be supported by virtue of the important work we do, don't project this bias when seeking funding.* Assuming that your corporate targets may lean to the

right of the political continuum, project yourself as someone seeking a business partnership to meet needs in the community.

7. *Develop your proposal by following the suggestions made in chapter 5.* This includes looking at your project from the corporation's perspective and asking yourself if it matches an allocation interest.

8. *Consider cause-related marketing as a possible way of receiving corporate dollars.* In brief, this refers to a corporation's relationship with a nonprofit "cause" that will somehow benefit the corporation through its association with you. It is usually more difficult for the smaller, lower profile agencies to form these partnerships.

Very profitable relationships do continue to be formed, however. An advantage of cause-related marketing is that funding may come from the corporation's advertising or marketing budget, rather than its charitable contributions budget.

9. *Ask your key board members to invite corporate leaders to serve on your board.* If you can identify, attract, and cultivate relationships with top management, these new board members will advocate for you within their corporations.[1]

The other advantage of having a board member from a top business is that he or she could have multiple resources to make a gift to your agency through a large salary, accumulated personal assets, or access to a charitable contributions budget or an advertising budget.

10. *In-kind services from corporations not only provide such advantages as free printing, meeting space, consultation, etc., but also an opportunity to form relationships.* A corporation that is sympathetic to your mission, but unable to fund your project, may be willing to extend other services to you. As your relationship develops, so will your chances for getting cash gifts in the future.

11. *Many corporations, especially those without a formal contributions department, will welcome a one- to two-page letter of request.* Although you don't need to be as comprehensive with

some corporations or businesses, you still need to be thoughtful in your presentation. I personally find it more difficult to write a short letter than a longer proposal. You have less margin for error and less room to make your case in a letter.

12. *Quiet persistence following a rejection will give you a better chance for funding in the future than kicking and screaming.* As Winston Churchill said, "Never give in, never give in, *never, never, never, never . . .*"

13. *The simplest, easiest way to find out what corporations are interested in is to ask them.* This is a blinding truth: it's so easy and obvious that we tend to miss it. Carve out a couple of days to sit down with your phone book, call every company you know, and ask them about their charitable interests. You should find common ground somewhere unless the only corporations in town are the general store and a gas station—even then you have a chance to find a match.

14. *Corporations, as well as foundations, want to know that your board members are actively involved in your fund-raising programs.* They figure, with good reason, that if those volunteers from the community who are closer to your agency than anyone else haven't invested themselves in raising money, why should they?

15. *The larger and more philanthropically active corporations in your area may be hesitant to "break the seal" by funding an agency that has not yet been supported by the corporate community.* Corporations will ask other corporations what they are doing for you. If a corporation's impulse to fund you is singular, if it is alone in the wilderness, you may not get the gift.

✳ ✳ ✳

Twenty years ago, a social service agency could be managed simply by the vision and energy of a charismatic administrator. To survive today, however, we need to borrow principles of successful business management to increase productivity and cost-effectiveness. Today, *change* is the bottom line.

Corporate philanthropy is *not* a contradiction in terms: it reflects the promise of new partnerships between the for-profit and nonprofit worlds that can result in at least raising the bottom for so many people in need throughout our nation.

7 How to Start a Wills and Bequests Program That Will Evolve into a Planned Gifts Program

I have enough money to last me the rest of my life, unless I buy something.

—Jackie Mason

Terms like *adjusted gross estate, gift annuities,* or *tangible personal property* make many human service providers numb. When I was first introduced to the technical aspects of planned giving, my eyes began to glass up somewhere between pooled income and charitable remainder unitrusts.

Few agencies have the resources to begin programs encouraging donor prospects to make a "planned" gift rather than an outright gift in their lifetimes. Such fund raising continues to be moved to the important-but-not-urgent pile while we go after outright gifts to meet the more urgent need to survive. Agencies need a simple way to begin a planned gift program, a way that leaves the staff with their hands free to raise money for present-day operations.

For those of you who are interested and ready, Appendix B provides a glossary of terms that will help you with the more sophisticated aspects of the Holy Grail of fund raising, planned giving. I also recommend that you select some of the reading material on the subject included in the Suggested Reading.

Now, for anyone else who has attended a half dozen seminars on planned giving and is still wondering how to get started, here's how:

A wills and bequests program that any agency can implement

1. We know that children learn things in sequence. We add and subtract before we multiply and divide. We learn the vocabulary of language before syntax. We walk before we run. The complexities of planned giving are virtually inaccessible to most smaller agencies. However, *we can begin a planned gift program by establishing a wills and bequests program first.*

2. *Identify your prospects.* The basic characteristic of a wills/ estate prospect is commitment to your agency or to your cause. Although our instincts might lure us into looking at our major donors for our top prospects, it is more likely that we will find estate gift prospects among those people who have been involved with our agency for a long time, possibly as a *volunteer or as a benefactor of your services* long ago. The volunteer who has walked to work for longer than you know or the part-time housekeeper you've employed for 20 years may very well be more inclined to remember you through an estate gift than your board president.

The other best source for an estate gift are *people who have been making small annual gifts to you for a long time.* These are people who have been *making gifts from their income* and finally reach the point in their lives where they are capable of *making a gift from their assets.* Get to know your long-term annual donors.

Assume that an individual who is not truly committed is

unlikely to make an estate gift. Marketing of our programs should be directed to those we believe have a high level of commitment to us. Past donors and longtime volunteers usually have this level of commitment.

Many prospects are mistakenly identified as such by their wealth, social status, influence, or the size of their contributions. Instead, the two best signs of commitment are regularity of giving and the length of time a person has been giving, regardless of the size of the gifts.

Keep in mind that people are living longer. More seniors mean more opportunities for wills and estate gifts. And baby boomers are aging. People don't start making gifts, as a rule of thumb, until they are in their late 40s. The boomers are presently in their early 40s. That's the good news. They're on their way. The bad news is that they are the ME generation and may not display the same philanthropic values of their parents.

3. *Ask board members to consider remembering your agency in their wills.* This will be a wake-up call for many.

4. *Consider asking your leadership staff to remember your agency in their wills.* This is even more important if you are not getting strong board leadership.

5. *Mail short, informational fliers to all the people on your list.* This is a good way to introduce wills/estate gifts in a new program or revive interest in an established one. Get the word out that you are seeking estate gifts. Let people know you need and value them. You don't have to spend a lot of money on this. Highly customized pieces will probably do no better in eliciting responses than material that is not customized. Regularity and consistency is important in communicating a wills and bequests program, so plan several mailings during the year.

6. *Send a personal letter and more information to those who respond.* Send a handwritten note to each person responding and enclose a brief flier that discusses estate planning more comprehensively. A tax attorney (if you have one on your board, so much the better) can help you design this. Then, make phone

contact with each person who has responded. Invite the prospect to visit your agency. Recommend that the prospect seek his or her own attorney to draft any legal documents regarding the gift. And ask for permission to publicly recognize the donor in future materials.

7. *Use your newsletter as a promotional device.* Revise the format and content of your newsletter so that it targets planned gift and major donor prospects. Do a feature story on anyone who has expressed an intention to name your agency in his or her will. Include a formal studio photograph of the donor. Send response envelopes that allow the people on your mailing list to ask for more information if they are interested.

8. *Conduct an estate planning seminar.* Invite your top prospects or donors to an estate planning presentation following dinner at your agency. To avoid concerns or competition that may arise, have the presentation made by a large bank or law firm in your area as opposed to a vendor who could be perceived as promoting his or her own financial product. It should be understood that the presenter will describe the importance of estate planning from a generic perspective and, also, how your agency could benefit by a planned gift.

9. *Present a donor and volunteer recognition evening.* Invite all of your top donors and volunteers to an annual appreciation dinner at your agency. Have someone give an inspirational speech thanking them for their efforts, award special gifts for top performances, and give everyone a certificate.

10. *Present planned gift seminars for your board members.* The purpose is to increase your board members' awareness of both the need for future money and the types of gift instruments available to acquire it.

11. *Inquire in your local community about the existence of nonprofit, planned gift organizations.* Many larger areas have planned gift associations that discuss planned gift instruments and marketing ideas monthly. Generally, the membership includes representatives from both the business community and

nonprofit agencies. *If there is a chapter in your community, I highly recommend your becoming a member of the National Planned Giving Council.*

Planned giving that will evolve from your wills and estate program

1. *After a donor has indicated an intention to make a bequest to your agency, cultivate a relationship with that person.* Trust is at the root of all good relationships and trust takes time to develop. Once you get to know donors better, they will be apt to divulge more information about their interests and goals. *Listen carefully to what your donors are saying.* You might learn that the donor is holding unneeded and valuable property but lacks life income, or you may learn that the donor is holding long term, highly appreciated stock that would be heavily taxed if sold.

Sympathize with the donor needs and look for win–win ways to meet those needs. In effect, you can expect the promotion around wills and estate gifts to introduce the notion of other planned giving arrangements such as trusts, annuities, gifts of life insurance, etc.

2. *The idea behind a planned gift program is to provide a broad range of gift opportunities to your prospects and donors while providing tax and other financial benefits such as passing assets on to heirs.*

3. *Convince your board of the need for a planned giving program.* This may be easier said than done, but do take steps to gain their support. One would think that this wouldn't be difficult. However, except for private sector professionals who regularly work with planned gift types of instruments—e.g., accountants, estate tax attorneys, stockbrokers, etc.,—*board members may be intimidated, bored, or confused if your program is not developed thoughtfully and presented clearly.*

4. There are basically three ways to make a "planned gift" to a charitable organization. As simply stated as possible, they are:

a. *bequests* (you receive all or a portion of the estate when the donor dies);
b. *annuities* (you receive money from the donor and then, based on standardized tables, pay the donor income until his/her death); and,
c. *trusts* (you receive money from the donor with assets flowing to the charity for its use upon fulfillment of the trust agreement).

5. *Establish a planned gift committee composed of trust officers, attorneys, brokers, insurance agents, and/or financial planners.*

6. *Don't build your planned gift program around life insurance plans.* Life insurance plans are seductive. The case sometimes goes, "Bob, we really have appreciated your annual gift of $300 over the last several years, but we'd like to ask you to consider turning that same $300 gift into a $30,000 gift by making us the owner and beneficiary of an insurance policy on your life . . ." Bob makes a gift to you every year and, since it is a gift, can take a tax deduction for it while you pay the annual premium with it. You own the cash value that accumulates, which you can borrow against, cash out if the donor lapses, or buy a smaller paid up policy on the donor's life.

One disadvantage of such a program is in its marketing. A common technique is to invite prospects from your donor list to, say, a dinner where the main speaker will be a life insurance agent. The agent will present an overview of insurance and how the gift works and you suggest that anyone interested in learning more about this opportunity talk to you after the meeting. Relationships with your top donors are jeopardized by the fact that you are not only introducing them to a sales-driven (rather than mission-driven) agent, but also by validating the agent by virtue of your sponsorship. It's tough to control for the potential bad results of this arrangement.

Another disadvantage is the likelihood of donor lapses resulting in either canceled or small paid up policies that need to be tracked for years.

Here are two exceptions to the caution about life insurance policies:

    a. A trusted board volunteer in the life insurance business can advise you regarding the cashing in of old paid up policies that are no longer needed by a donor—e.g., he or she has accumulated other assets along the way.

    b. If you can live with the life insurance agents who are likely to come out of the woodwork when you begin to talk about introducing a program, a life insurance program can be a useful *supplementary* source of extra income.

7. *A donor can make a gift to your agency and keep the right to life income and get some tax benefits, too.* Donors can do this through annuities (current pay or deferred pay and trust arrangements—i.e., annuity and universal).

8 Public Relations and Special Events

*In this and like communities, public sentiment is
   everything.*
With public sentiment, nothing can fail;
without it nothing can succeed.

—Abraham Lincoln

The story goes that Albert Einstein went from town to town with his chauffeur giving talks on his theory of relativity. One day the chauffeur said, "You know, Albert, I've heard you talk about relativity so many times, I think I could do one of your presentations myself!" To this Einstein said, "You know, that's not a bad idea . . . let's swap clothes and *you* do the talk and I'll pretend to be your driver."

So, at the next town, the chauffeur went on stage and described the theory as Einstein sat near the podium in uniform. After the applause died down, however, a man in the front row asked a very complex question about time and space.

After a moment, the quick-thinking chauffeur said, "Now that is a very thoughtful and difficult question. However," he said, gesturing to Einstein, "the answer is actually so remarkably simple that even my chauffeur can answer it . . ."

I feel somewhat like the chauffeur in describing public relations activities and special events as these have long been a speciality of human and social service agencies. However, let me exchange uniforms for awhile to make a few points.

Special events

1. *Conduct one special event a year, but frame it as a public relations activity rather than as a fund-raising activity.* Special events take an enormous amount of time and energy to conduct and there is no assurance that you will make much money on them. You may set yourself up for failure if your primary objective in conducting a special event is to raise a lot of money.

Here is a hypothetical story of two agencies:

a. The Institute for Single Parent Fathers decided to have a *special event*, a formal dinner dance, to raise money.

It was a father–daughter event and its main objective was to raise $20,000. A committee planned it for a year, nearly 250 people showed up, and they got a big story and photograph in the newspaper, but only raised $12,000. The volunteer leaders were discouraged and most of them didn't work on it again the following year.

b. On the other hand, the Society of Myopic Adults decided to conduct a *public relations activity*, a formal dinner dance, the following year. The members had two major objectives: they wanted to increase their profile in the community and they wanted to attract potential donors and new volunteers to the society.

At the dinner dance, one year later, nearly 250 people showed, they got a big story and photograph in the newspaper, and were elated to have not only met their two main goals, but also raised $12,000 to boot! All the volunteers were energized and excited about planning for the next event now that they had this experience under their belts.

If you frame your special event as, primarily, a fund raiser, others may say to you that special events are too much work and raise too little money. It's interesting, though, how much more support special events receive when they have these objectives, instead, in descending order of importance:

- Meet people who can help you someday.
- Promote a positive image of your agency in the community,—i.e., get some positive attention in the newspaper, radio, television, etc.
- Raise some money.

2. As soon as you are confident enough in the volunteer committee providing the leadership of a special event, give the committee the space to develop its own life. *In other words, don't attend their planning meetings.* You will be less likely to get entangled in the relationship difficulties that *all* committees will have from time to time.

Of course, the committee will need your guidance and control if it's your first event, but, even then, remove yourself from attendance as early as possible. The secret of making this committee an effective and inexpensive fund-raising resource lies in your relationship with its chairperson. If he or she communicates openly and regularly with you, you will be much better able to mediate and motivate during the rough spots.

3. To decrease the chances of sponsoring a bust event, *give all special event* **ideas** *generous time to incubate.* We discussed the possibility of conducting a golf outing, on and off, for two years. When we finally decided to proceed, we took another 18 months to plan it. The caution was worth it because it not only got positive press and attracted new board members to Parmadale, we enjoyed a triple-figure net profit as well.

4. Although having a volunteer chairperson who is connected to influential members of the community is a plus, lean toward *people who will work rather than lend their names only.*

5. The chairperson needs to take pains to ensure that *everyone has a task that matches his or her inclinations and skills.* We should master the art of volunteer jujitsu and surrender to volunteers' individual strengths rather than try to force them to fit into our own preconceived expectations.

Public relations

We have relations with the public whether or not we have a public relations program and we have an image in the community whether or not we try to do anything to influence that image. One might think that no local human or social service agency can have too high a profile in the community assuming it's a positive one. But a high profile also makes an easy-to-hit target.

Assuming, though, that you are less concerned with becoming too well known and more with controlling the perception your various publics have of your agency whenever you can, here are a few steps you can take.

1. *Identify your publics.* You have internal and external publics. Your internal publics include your board of trustees and key staff. Your external publics include consumers, or people and agencies who buy your programs and/or services, suppliers and vendors, prospects and donors, politicians, the business community, and the general community. This list will be different for each of us, but these publics should make sense for most of us.

2. *Identify and examine actual or potential misperceptions of each public especially noting those that could ultimately have a significant negative impact on you.* Parmadale used to be an orphanage and some people think that it still is. Although this is a misperception, it is not one that is likely to hurt us. On the other hand, some people assume that the children we care for are dangerous to the community. This misperception is not only far from the truth: it is potentially harmful.

3. *Next, develop a proactive plan of individual strategies for shaping your image with each of these publics.* For example, if you think that board members are less aware than they should be about what's going on in your programs, you could invite key staff to make presentations at the beginning of each board meeting.

If you think board members are too naive about or resistant to fund raising, you could plan to increase the availability of written literature for board members, bring in a recognized professional fund raiser from outside the organization to discuss expectations, and encourage attendance of key board members at appropriate development seminars conducted in the community. You could also purchase subscriptions to fund-raising magazines for the members of your development committee.

If you need to improve your image with people or agencies that purchase your services, you could develop and mail a new agency brochure, invite key leadership for dinner and a videotape presentation, develop or strengthen your newsletter, start a speaker's bureau and present seminars in your area of expertise, or invite key people to your agency for talks and tours.

If you want to improve your image with the general public send query letters to editors of newspapers and magazines inviting them to either do a feature or consider a staff-written article, develop 10- and 30-second spot public service announcements (PSAs) for radio, enlist the local high school communications department to do a television spot as part of a class project, send your logo and slogan to local cable television bulletin boards, and offer an open house for neighbors.

A thoughtful public relations program will increase positive feelings about your agency, clarify the true nature of your mission, encourage the positive images that are currently held, and improve internal relationships with staff and board members.

The way to approach doing these things, with no staff and little money, is to use your volunteers, especially in the area of distribution of materials,—i.e., actually carrying your message to the public.

4. The short list of *critical materials that you need to develop for fund raising* includes:

    a. an attractive, readable newsletter,

    b. at least one good agency flier,

    c. a case statement loaded with anecdotes that volunteers can tell and retell, and,

    d. a powerful appeal letter.

The basic copy for all of these is within our own capacity to create, although a volunteer with writing skills can certainly help.

If you have the resources, other helpful activities include placing PSAs on radio/television, appearing on radio and television talk shows, doing print advertising, presenting slide shows, and setting up display booths at local malls.

5. We all know that a positive two-minute television or radio spot, aired some time other than between 2 a.m. and 6 a.m., gives us much more exposure than a ton of fliers and brochures. The question is, how do we get it? Here are some ideas:

    a. *Invite a local television anchor to speak at or emcee your special event.* The station will send a camera crew out to tape it.

    b. *Invite the talent from more than one station;* you'll get a better response.

    c. *When you inform the promotions officer of a station about a special event you have coming up, mention that you expect the other stations to cover it.* Keep in mind that the primary motivation of the people at the station's assignment desk is to beat the competition.

    d. *Sunday is a good time to break a television story because it's usually a dead day for local news.*

    e. *Find out when the ratings sweeps are in your area,—e.g., January, February, May, July, October, and November— and submit story ideas at least six weeks in advance.* Prior to the sweeps, television and radio people are aggressively searching for good story leads.

f. *Because our stories are soft news, we have to find an angle that will hook the viewer.* Would you be interested in hearing about an 80-year-old volunteer who walked three miles to an agency twice a week? Would you be more interested if I told you that she skateboarded there? How about if I told you that she came in second in the 80+ division of the regional skateboarding competition and that she probably would have won it if she hadn't been up half the night playing darts?

9 How to Conduct a Capital Campaign

The rare individual who unselfishly tries to serve others has an enormous advantage. He has little competition.

—Dale Carnegie

Bob and John, fund raisers for two different social service agencies, went on a camping trip together. At dawn, a huge bear began to prowl their camp. Bob started to put on his tennis shoes and John said, "Why are you putting on your tennis shoes? You can't outrun a bear!" To this Bob calmly replied, "I don't have to outrun the bear . . . I just have to outrun you."

Over the past several years at Parmadale, my boss, our board, and I have worn through many pairs of sneakers trying to outrun our competition.

Without previous experience, an established constituency, or the support of a paid consultant, we raised more than $1.2 million in three years for Parmadale. The successful completion of the campaign lead us to another $2 million state grant and a $600,000 private match two years later.

The suggestions made in this chapter are based on the encouragement that came from our little successes along the way and the failures that were our greatest teachers.

The problems

When we began, words and phrases like solicitation or major donor prospect were simply not in our vocabulary. We didn't just start from scratch, we didn't even arrive at scratch until about six months into the campaign. The bear outside our camp was formidable.

1. Our most obvious drawback was that not only had we never conducted a capital campaign, we had never done individual fund raising of any kind. Besides foundations and government entities, none of us had ever asked anyone for money.

2. Although we had served nearly 100,000 people over the last 65 years as a residential child-care treatment center, our "graduates" didn't choose to attend Parmadale as an alumnus of Harvard would have chosen to attend Harvard. In fact, we only had records of 38 people who made a gift the year before we started our campaign. We had an extremely small base of individual constituents.

3. Like many smaller nonprofits throughout the country, we receive funds from a local United Way Services. Although these monies are vital for the continued provision of our quality services, we had been historically restricted from developing funding partnerships with major local corporations.

4. We had a "working" board that was composed of educators, public officials, and human service professionals. We had no one on our board of great wealth or great community influence. Further, no board member ever expected to have to make a cash gift to Parmadale.

We assumed that if we paid for an outside consultant to conduct a formal feasibility study, these factors would emerge as reasons we should not proceed. What we believed couldn't be fully factored in—that if this building was not built soon, many children would suffer.

The guidelines

Consider these steps if you are thinking about trying to outrun the bear and raise capital money.

1. *Conduct your own feasibility study.* Here's how we conducted ours:

> My boss said, "We need to raise a million dollars to construct a building." I said, "I don't think we're ready." He said, "You're probably right, let's do it anyway."

This is not to imply there isn't an advantage in doing a sophisticated feasibility study. There is. For one thing, you learn how much support you have in advance of "going public" and, by framing your interviews with key prospects as "nonsolicitations," you can get information without the stress that comes from actually asking for money face-to-face.

However, at Parmadale, we concluded that small social service agencies will never "be ready," not when readiness is defined in comparison to the colleges and cultural organizations that have been raising money for decades.

How do you reconcile this need for information, on one hand, with compelling need to proceed with your project on the other? I suggest that one way to do this is to conduct your own informal feasibility study.

Develop a list of key people in your community, people like bankers, realtors, attorneys, CEOs, etc. Send them a letter asking if they would give a 20-minute interview to a volunteer on your board. Promise you won't ask them for money. Write some questions like, "Do you think the community would support our campaign?" or, "What kind of public image do we have?" Conduct the same interview with all of your volunteers. You will gain good information and make some new friends. The rule of thumb is that no matter how many people you talk to, you will have a pretty good idea of your campaign's potential after talking to only five people.

2. *Learn everything you can about the capital campaign process.*

Assuming that you can't afford $20,000 a month for a prestigious fund-raising company to come in and run your campaign for you, you will need to learn as much about the capital campaign process as you can. As I had done many years earlier as a rookie English teacher, I stayed "a chapter ahead of the kids" this way.

Talk to anyone you can find who has been involved with a campaign. Someone whose campaign failed may be as valuable as someone who has succeeded. Secretaries can give you insights that you can't buy out of Chicago. Join your local fund-raising organization if one exists. Subscribe to magazines. Go to your library.

Shop for a full-time development director who is not a consultant, but who, for a small fee, will gladly sit down with you for a couple of days and share his or her insights. An investment of a few hundred dollars will pay big dividends.

Attend workshops. Drag along, even if they're kicking and screaming, any key players you would think would also benefit from the workshop. For example, bring your board development chairperson to a seminar on the role of the volunteer. This will help neutralize the potential "Nazarene in the hometown" effect that can happen as you acquire some knowledge in the area.

3. *Identify your volunteer leadership.* Make this a top priority.

4. *Share ownership of the capital campaign with your board.* For your capital campaign to be successful, ownership of the campaign absolutely must be shared among the director of the agency, key board members, and whoever you have on staff to help you raise money.

5. *Insist on 100 percent gift support from your board members.* This isn't a guideline. It's a rule.

6. *Write your proposal.* Write it right. Your proposal is argua-

bly the most important single tool for your whole campaign. Follow the outline described in chapter 5.

Keep it brief. Enhance main points in the appendix for those readers who may want more information.

The actual proposal-writing process will force you to think strategically and carefully about the project. Next, the proposal will become your marketing tool and, finally, after you have reached your goal, the proposal will become your blueprint for implementation or, in some instances, even your contract.

7. *Plan on spending some money.* Depending upon such variables as the size of your campaign goal, number of active major donors in your constituency, visibility in the community, and local economic factors, you can expect to spend between twelve and twenty cents on a dollar.

8. *Identify your prospects.* Develop a firm list of all of the organizations and individuals you know who might contribute to your campaign. Involve your board volunteers in the process. This is how we divided ours:

a. board members
b. staff
c. private and community foundations
d. corporate foundations
e. businesses that don't have formal philanthropic divisions
f. individuals who might give a major gift and give early in the campaign
g. individuals who, collectively, would make many small gifts

Consider government sources, too. As a general rule, many social service agencies overestimate the amount of support they expect from corporations.

9. *Go after your major gifts first.* The Pareto Principle, or 80/20 rule, suggests that 20 percent of your donors will give you 80 percent of your money. Major donors like to be asked early, in the beginning of a campaign.

10. *Plan the "public" portion of your fund raising for the end of your campaign.* Don't expect to raise much money this way.

Your campaign should be nearly completed before you "go public."

11. *Develop your materials.* You will need at least the following materials for public distribution.

    a. proposal
    b. short-form of your proposal
    c. agency flier
    d. capital campaign flier
    e. pledge cards
    f. mailing and return envelopes
    g. posters (optional)
    h. brief video presentation (optional)

12. *Create a headquarters for the campaign.* Depending upon the size and resources of the agency, designate some space to run your campaign. Whether or not you have a fund-raising staff, someone will have to keep accurate records of:

    a. who has been solicited
    b. who made the solicitations
    c. who made a gift and for how much
    d. who has been thanked
    e. who does and doesn't want public recognition
    f. who has made a pledge and when that person wants to be reminded to pay it.

You will need to generate reports for volunteer team members (to keep them accountable and motivated), foundation sources, and your auditors. If you can't hire a temporary bookkeeper during the public portion of your campaign, help your present clerical staff divest some responsibilities to enable them to handle the considerable minutiae in store for you.

13. *Ask people for money.* Most campaigns fail because staff and board, new to the game, don't ask enough people for money. This is particularly true of smaller social service agencies that have traditionally relied upon government support. Don't make the mistake of doing everything else well, except asking.[1]

14. *Divide the job of asking among members of your team.* At Parmadale, we succeeded with this formula:

The *director* devoted much of his time to acquiring an advance gift, a gift that turned out to be the single largest gift of the campaign.

Board members broke new ground by raising money both from individuals and corporations.

The *development director* did all the foundation submissions and was responsible for campaign management.

15. *Use the "group of 12" method of board solicitation.* This is a simple (but not easy) way to help volunteers raise money. Here are the steps:

   a. Identify the 12 wealthiest and most influential people you know who you think would join a committee to help your campaign succeed.
   b. Have the "right person" (or persons) on your board ask these 12 to help. The right person is someone to whom the prospect finds it difficult to say no to.
   c. Tell members that you will have eight one-hour meetings over the next year and that attendance is extremely important.
   d. Tell members that they have two responsibilities: make a gift early and raise a specific amount of money from others.
   e. Tell members that they will report their progress at every meeting.

The secret to the success of this method is in reaching as high as you can for the first member of this elite group. He or she will attract the rest of the group.

16. *Create a time line.* Next, give yourself extra time. Done? Now go back and give yourself more extra time. The task of raising capital will be stressful enough without the additional burden of an unrealistic, self-imposed time line.

17. *Use volunteers to help you do foundation research.*

18. *Make sure that you send out a thank you within 48 hours*

of receiving a gift. I once told my boss that my job could be reduced to saying two things: "thank you" and "I'm sorry." This simplification points to the importance of doing cultivation work for the future. You will attract many new donors to your campaign. Think past the campaign conclusion and remember that most of these donors will become regular, sustaining contributors if they are properly cultivated. A prompt and personal thank you is a first step.

Consider writing your thank you to top donors in long hand. When was the last time you failed to read a letter to you that was written by hand? Also, a personal phone call should be made as soon as you receive what you define as a large gift.

19. *Make sure that all the players on your team know what is expected from them.* Board volunteers and staff should know precisely what their roles and tasks are. Be candid in the beginning.

20. *Give everyone specific, concrete and measurable objectives.* Volunteers, especially, should know the answer to these questions:

   a. What do you want me to do?
   b. When do you want me to do it by?
   c. When I'm done, how will I know whether I succeeded?

21. *Provide training to staff and volunteers.* Because capital campaigns are periodic activities, very few organizations, even colleges, have people on staff who are experts. Money that goes to provide good training experiences will be well spent.

22. *Accept the fact that most successful campaigns will demand up to 40 percent of the director's time and 95 percent of your fund-raising staff's time.* All staff must communicate regularly about campaign developments and volunteers will need more of your time than ever before.

Hidden benefits to your agency

After you've successfully completed your campaign and cleared your head from the few whacks you'll be sure to take along the way, you will discover these extra benefits:

1. *You will have an enlarged constituency.* You will have new donors who will become future annual donors. New foundation benefactors and corporate sponsors will also emerge.

2. *You will have raised your volunteers' fund-raising consciousness to new heights.* New volunteers will emerge as leaders while you weed out those members who aren't prepared to invest themselves, financially, in your future.

3. *You will have a much higher profile in your community.* With work and any kind of luck, the media attention you will have received will help future fund-raising efforts.

As you begin your own campaign, remember that you can't do everything at once, but you can do something at once. Why not start by lacing up your running shoes?

10 Burn, Burned, Burnt: The Conjugation of a Fund Raiser

Ask not what your agency can do for you, ask what you can do for your agency.

—Unknown

Fund raising can be a draining profession. The prospect of providing direct services to people in pain, managing an agency that is in a survival gear, and introducing the new responsibilities of raising money continues to discourage agency directors from even trying.

Have you heard about the doctor who told the guy he has bad news and worse news? The doctor said, "The bad news is that your test reports just came back and you only have 24 hours to live." The guy responded, "Well, what could the worse news be?" The doctor replied, "I tried to call you yesterday."

In terms of stress and fund raising, though, I have good news and bad news. The good news is that fund raising can't make you crazy. The bad news is that your attitude about it can.

This chapter suggests how to raise friends and money without going crazy.

1. We have one of the most easily *measurable* activities in the nonprofit world. We're extremely accountable. Our job is to raise money.

We treat kids at Parmadale, kids who have serious problems. But, if we simply help a kid get old at Parmadale, or survive, we can still take credit for helping him. Not so in fund raising. We either raise the money and make our goals or we don't.

So, one source of stress is trying to raise money in competitive and increasingly more challenging economic times.

2. For many reasons, some of us have overadapted to our jobs. Our need for security and stability, in such an unpredictable profession as ours, tends to drive us too hard. We overadapt to our careers. In short, we become in conflict with ourselves. We are especially at risk when we become too attached to our careers as our *primary* source of fulfillment.

If I were to identify the things I value most in life, work would be no higher than fourth or fifth on my list, but often demands the most and the best of my time and energy. We have a *goal conflict* if we want to rise to the top of our fields by working weekends and evenings, *and* spend a lot of time with our families.[1]

3. In regard to *the development of relationships*, I believe that the following four statements both define a formula for our success and reflect a great source of role stress. Much stress, incidentally, comes from the various hats we wear, the roles we play. We are fathers, mothers, husbands, daughters, disciplinarians, lovers, employees, employers, fund raisers, etc.

The four statements are:

a. Our success as fund raisers depends on good relationships.
b. Good relationships take time to develop.
c. People come and go in our profession—staff, board members, other volunteers, donors, people come and go.
d. While these people are coming and going, we still have to raise money.

I've never had any luck meeting a guy on a golf course on Tuesday and calling him on Wednesday and saying, "Would you consider making a $10,000 gift to our capital campaign?" . . . *I've done it!* . . . I've just never had any luck with it. Good relationships take time, but we don't always have enough of it.

4. The next time you have that dreaded feeling of angst and can't put your finger on the problem, change the question from "what's the matter with me?" to *"who's the matter with me?"* Since we have so many activities going on at the same time, it's sometimes difficult to localize problems. Our stress becomes all-pervasive: the edges of our tasks blur. We have a feeling of unfocused self-criticism.

Remember, at times like this, that most stress-related problems in development revolve around *relationships* and I submit that the most stressful relationships we have in fund raising are between ourselves and our immediate supervisor, key board member, or key major donor prospect.

Further, I would bet that potentially the absolute most stressful relationship of all is with your own boss.

You can have a great day and, on your way out, your boss says something critical. You'll stew about it all night. Or you can have a terrible day, when nothing goes right, and just as you leave, your boss takes a moment to tell you how much he appreciates you. You feel like a million bucks all night.

5. *Unresolved, serious values conflicts will drive you out of the field.* For example, we may become rigidly fixed upon reaching our goals and come to repress feelings of self-betrayal around the little compromises we make when our personal values contradict the values of our organization.

Some examples of values conflicts are:

a. You can't stand being asked for money over the phone and you're curt or nasty to a cold caller, yet you direct a phone campaign.

b. You are appalled by the reality of conspicuous consumption in our society but are the chief staff supporter of a black-tie dinner dance at a swank hotel.

6. *Define roles and expectations clearly.* Your institution's top staff, volunteers, and you should have a clear understanding of your respective roles and expectations. Without these understandings, you will end up projecting blame when things get tough. Ownership of the responsibility for raising money should be mutually shared.

7. A classic symptom of fund raiser burnout is the loss of charisma. I suggest that you *don't fly too close to the sun.* Following an extended period high-flying, high-energy campaign, you may begin to doubt yourself. You may perceive that those around you have become disappointed because the "miracles" they expected you to perform have not materialized. If this is the case, make an emergency landing and take a good look at yourself. Plan to reach your goal on foot rather than by air: become a long-distance runner instead of a jet pilot.

8. *Refuse to recycle a negative thought or feeling.* If a board member, say, criticizes you unfairly on Tuesday, that's HIS problem. But if you're still upset about it on Friday, that's YOUR problem. Resentment comes from the Latin root *sentire,* which means *to feel.* Resentment means to re-feel a real or imagined injury to your pride or ego. You refuse to let it go. You stew over it and take it out to lunch. You fuel it. You can't control the many external stressors that you'll experience in fund raising, but you can choose how you will react.

Negative thoughts will die a natural death if you refuse to energize them with your attention by mulling them over and over in your mind.

In the play *Antigone,* Ismene said, "I have no desire to suffer twice: once in reality and once in retrospect."

A cartoon I saw some time ago of an elderly lady at a gravesite filled with flowers expresses to what extremes we can go in holding onto a resentment. She smiles up at her companion and says, "Oh, I come here every day, he always hated flowers."

9. *Develop a healthy realism about your skills and get as much training as you can.* Our incompetence stresses us. No one

knows everything there is to know about fund raising. Generalists play a GOOD game in most of the big areas and specialists play a GREAT game in a few. Fund raisers rarely are experts at everything, however. If we secretly believe that we don't have the skills to accomplish our objectives, we'll cope with great feelings of inadequacy. You begin to fix this when you decide to become a life-long student of the art.

10. It's in your own long-term best interest, and the best interest of your team, *to set attainable goals*. Volunteers who fail will tend to be one-timers. Staff who chronically fail leave the field. The constant pressure to raise more and more money is our eternal reality. Given scarce resources, however, unrealistic goals defeat us. There is a thin line between goals that push us to excel and goals that push us toward burnout.

11. *Learn to integrate and keep track of a great deal of information*. We have to manage multiple priorities. One of the challenges in our field is to focus clearly on one diverse task after another, even when the tasks call for different skills. Some days, we need to be an accountant during a breakfast meeting, a creative writer later in the morning, a mediator between angry volunteers at lunch, a cheerleader with our staff in the afternoon, and a strategic planner with our evening development committee.

Here's a technique that won't teach you how to play your various parts, but at least will help you remember what your lines are:

    a. Write everything down. As the proverb goes, the palest ink is stronger than the best memory.

    b. Rank your list.

    c. Schedule when you will work on your priorities.

    d. Act.

Here's another:

Delegate whenever you can. If you have been doing everything you can and delegating the rest, you're on the wrong track. Instead, delegate everything you can, and do only what no one else can do.

12. *Become an active member of a good professional organization of fund raisers.* It is the perception of some that fund raisers and snake oil salesmen are cut from the same cloth. Damage to your self-esteem from these negative and stereotypical attitudes can be aggravated by the perception or reality of low status within your organization. Some of us work in a vacuum, isolated from others who are doing the same kind of work.

An important influence on our mental health is the development of friends and colleagues outside of institutions.

13. *Insist on periods of solitude for yourself.* We have infrequent and all too brief grace periods. The relief we experience following the news that our proposal has been funded has a life span of about 36 hours at Parmadale. Take time to empty yourself of the noises of the day. Renew yourself with quiet.

Create untouchable times daily, weekly, monthly, and annually. For example, set aside a half hour a day, two hours a week, one day a month, one week a year, just to get your interior world back into perspective. Write these times on your calendar and consider them booked. I went on a one-day retreat a month ago, all by myself, and it was wonderful.

14. *Practice being a team-player.* Many fund raisers are creative people who are talented in one or more of the language, visual, or musical arts. This is good for our institutions, but it can be personally frustrating. A leading violinist said that one of the things she likes most is the fact that she is in *total control* of her music when she performs. As a painter (I do portrait art), I wouldn't think of handing the brush to someone else for "input" and some writers give editors headaches over changing a semicolon to a comma.

The fact that we don't have complete control over our creative work, the work of fund raising, can be a major source of stress.

Successful fund raising is achieved by teamwork. With few

exceptions, fund raising is not for the brooding and solitary artist who cannot or will not bond with others.

15. *Learn how to reduce conflict in relationships.* Once you have identified the person you are in conflict with, be proactive in trying to reduce tension. Remind yourself that if there's a winner when the conflict is over, it isn't over.

16. *Practice acceptance.* When we are overworked and over-tired and not yet achieving our fund-raising goals, we become inclined to push ourselves to work even harder. Unfortunately, the multiple demands of fund-raising environments don't usually relent in the face of sheer force of will: the harder we seem to work, the more frustrated we become. Our frustration can turn into exhaustion and cynicism and we become less effective in accomplishing our goals.

Learn to swing at the fast balls and not the curve balls and accept the fact that you're not going to get a base hit every time you go to the plate.

Use theologian Reinhold Nieburh's *Serenity Prayer,* "God give us grace to accept with serenity the things that cannot be changed, courage to change the things which should be changed and the wisdom to distinguish the one from the other." I don't think we need much more than this . . .

17. *Don't borrow trouble from the future.* As fund raisers, we are verbs not nouns. We are constantly moving toward a point in the distance. We plan, develop, motivate, cajole, harangue, and guide—all words that imply future action. Practice the principle of living one day at a time. Better yet, stay in the present moment because that's where all the action is. Avoid chronic anticipation because, as Gertrude Stein said, "When you get there, there isn't any there there."

18. *Accept the fact that rejection is unpleasant but temporary and that each rejection moves you closer to your goal.* Asking for money is confrontative. We risk rejection every time we ask for money ourselves or motivate others to ask for money.

We'll become more resilient to rejection by keeping our

mission clearly in mind. Remind yourself that you are advocating for a cause much larger than you. Hang your ego up with your hat and find your energy in the confidence that comes from knowing you are helping your institution achieve its goals.

Try desensitization exercises. List all of the singular, small steps that lead up to and through a solicitation, for example. Next, visualize each step in a relaxed frame of mind. Do this over and over until you can imagine the scene without setting off all types of tension provoking triggers.

For objectivity, bring in an outside consultant to train staff and volunteers in the solicitation process. Then, practice and role play what you have learned.

Develop a strong support system between staff and board members. Discuss your solicitation experiences and keep each other's spirits up.

19. *Slouching toward fund raising.* As a talented development professional, you attract work. More than likely, you tend to take on too much work and work too intensely. You become immobilized when you take on too much. For folks who hear *no* often enough, we aren't very good at saying *no* to others. Set limits on yourself. Although we like to blame others for our work load, our "can-do" attitude is often responsible for our crossing the line between challenging and unattainable objectives.

20. *Remember that venting is different from calling for action.* Make it easier for your boss to support you by agreeing to identify your expressions of concern as either a "vent" or a "call for action." If you're so upset that you can't tell whether you just need to get something off your chest or need a change, give your boss permission to make the call.

21. Some guy said to me once, "You want to know how to reduce stress? I'll tell you how to reduce stress. Raise money, that's how." And he's right. Joe Louis said, "It's not that I like money, it's just that it quiets my nerves." Sophie Tucker said, "I have been poor and I've been rich. Rich is better." Raising

money certainly reduces stress for awhile just as not raising money increases stress for awhile.

But, there's an ambush here, and it's this: after a successful solicitation, I would find myself talking like the guy in the commercial . . . "I can do that, I can do that," and I tended during those times to set unrealistic, grandiose goals. Conversely, after some defeats, I would lose confidence in my ability to raise a dime. The point is that we should set all of our goals, financial or otherwise, remembering that *feelings are not facts*. Avoid making ANY major life decisions when we are too angry, too frightened, too sad, or too glad.

*   *   *

In summary, it is not the "things that happen to us" in fund raising, but our perceptions, beliefs, and what we tell ourselves about what happens to us that cause us emotional distress. According to Marcus Aurelius, "If you are pained by an external thing, it is not this thing that disturbs you, but your own judgment about it. And it is in your power to wipe out this judgment now."

It is in our power to change our attitudes about the stresses of our profession. However, willingness is a much more important ingredient in the stress-reduction equation than is self-knowledge. We can read everything in print about coping better, but if we aren't willing to *change*, this information won't do us any good.

Coping with stress in fund raising may mean *changing* your attitude and/or behavior. However, solutions are seldom arrived at when you are under severe stress. Stress makes us tighten up and become rigid and inflexible when what is needed is flexibility of thought. And, change itself is stressful.

Therefore, assuming you are not currently in a crisis state, now is the time to take some preventive steps. Remember, there is only one thing more painful than learning from experience, and that is *not* learning from experience. Also, remember that you don't have to be sick to get better.

Appendix A
Internal Development Audit

This audit offers an accounting of phrases that allude to the various resources that are generally necessary to establish and develop a successful fund-raising program in a small to midsize human services agency. The audit isn't scientific; it's intended to give you a brief overview of the main points, the critical components, of a well-rounded fund-raising program. For those of you like myself, though, who are disappointed if you don't find a little scorecard at the end of a survey, you will find a rating code at the end.

Rate each area with the code:
— 5   No problem; we have it covered
— 4   Good job; room for improvement
— 3   Fair job; needs attention and energy
— 2   Weak; barely scratching the surface
— 1   We've been thinking about starting to do this . . . maybe
— 0   We have to do **this,** too?

Organizational

— Mission statement
— Needs assessment

__ Case statement
__ Fund-raising action plan
__ Regularly scheduled communications
__ Volunteer teams
__ Realistic and attainable goals
__ Willingness and capacity to change
__ Development committee
__ Fund-raising staff

Board Development

__ Members who have wealth and power
__ Expectation that they need to make a gift and ask others for money
__ One hundred percent annual gift support
__ Shared ownership between agency director, staff and board
__ Opportunity for training and support
__ Process in place for prospect identification and recruitment

Major Gifts

__ Strong composition of volunteers regularly asking for the gift
__ Process in place to identify and cultivate major donor prospects
__ Right person being recruited to ask for the gift
__ Opportunity for training and support
__ Recognition program in place
__ Volunteer development

Annual Fund

__ Acquisition mailings
__ Upgraded donor mailings
__ Creative letter writing
__ Prospect research

__ Gift clubs
__ Telephone campaigns
__ Membership drives
__ Volunteer development
__ Recognition program in place

Grantsmanship

__ Understanding of construction of proposal
__ Capacity to write persuasive proposals
__ Understanding of how to research foundations
__ Good foundation relations

Corporate Philanthropy

__ Understanding of limitations and opportunities
__ Cause related marketing
__ Key corporate leaders involved as volunteers
__ In-kind services
__ Research process in place

Wills and Estates Program

__ Identified prospects
__ Board members, key staff leaving agency in will
__ Information mailings
__ Face-to-face presentations made
__ Emphasis in newsletter; donor profiles
__ Estate planning seminars
__ Life insurance as supplemental resource

Public Relations and Marketing

__ Radio and television PSAs
__ Regular distribution of agency flier to donors and prospects

__ Special events geared to increase profile
__ Video tapes, slide shows
__ Print advertising
__ Public speaking at civic, church groups, etc.
__ Reactive plan in place in case of unexpected negative publicity
__ Target population identified
__ Intermediate and long term goals established
__ Positioning strategy conducted
__ Printed materials including newsletter, agency flier, solicitation materials

Special Events

__ At least one annual special event conducted that both raises money and increases positive image in community

Capital Campaign

__ Feasibility study
__ Volunteer leadership committed
__ Development of case statement
__ Development of proposal
__ Prospect identification
__ Organization of campaign divisions
__ Advanced gifts/Board gifts
__ Major gifts
__ Foundations
__ Corporations
__ Government
__ Public
__ Printed materials
__ Realistic timelines established

* * *

Add up your scores and divide by 73. Rate yourself in the following manner:

5.0–4.1   You're in great shape. Remember that you don't have to be sick, though, to get better. Beware of the status quo. Push yourself to continue to change because if you don't grow, you go.

4.0–3.1   You're a pace-setter doing more with less. Concentrate on developing yourself in those areas you scored weakest on and that common sense tells you are most critical to your success.

3.0–2.1   You have a good start toward successful fund raising. Remember that your investment in hard work, continued education and good volunteers will bring great returns.

2.0–1.1   You have some work in front of you, but you're in good company because, unfortunately, many human service agencies are only now beginning to see the need and importance for aggressive fund raising.

1.0–0.0   Well, the good news is that there's nowhere else to go but up!

Appendix B

Glossary of Planned Giving Terms

Appreciated property

An asset that has increased in value and which would produce a capital gain if sold at its fair market value. This vehicle for outright giving allows the donor to receive a gift deduction for the current market value while avoiding paying tax on the capital gains.

Bargain sale

A donor may sell property or other marketable assets to you and receive only partial payment. The difference between the market value and the actual payment is considered a gift and can be deducted according to bargain sale regulations.

Charitable gift annuity

This form of gift pays life income to the donor in exchange for assets such as cash or securities. You guarantee income for one or two lives. The donor also receives an income tax deduction based upon the age or ages of the income beneficiaries.

Charitable lead trust

There are several types of lead trusts that allow the donor to make gifts from his or her income to your agency for a period of years after which the value of the trust is either returned to the donor or the donor's heirs.

Charitable remainder annuity trust

This type of trust pays a fixed amount over a specified period to one or more individuals and then, at the end of the period, distributes the remainder of its assets to your agency.

Charitable remainder unitrust

This is the same as a *charitable remainder annuity trust*, except that a fixed percentage, determined annually, is paid on the unitrust value.

Codicil

A codicil is an addition to an existing will.

Deferred gift

A deferred gift provides an immediate tax advantage to the donor and a future gift benefit to your agency.

Gift of home with life residency

It is possible for the donor to give your agency a home while retaining the right to live in the home for life. A charitable income tax deduction, calculated based upon the age or ages of the residents, can be taken by the donor who arranges the gift.

Life insurance

Donors can give an existing policy to your agency and receive an income tax deduction for the value of the policy as determined by the life insurance company. Donors may purchase a new policy and if your agency is named as both owner and beneficiary, the donor may take a deduction for premiums paid. Consult experts in your state for local information on gifts of new life insurance policies for charitable causes.

Planned gift

A planned gift can be a single gift or a combination of several types of gifts that enable a donor to give a larger gift than would otherwise be possible. A planned gift generally implies a need for some measure of financial, legal or tax planning.

Pooled income fund

A pooled income fund is a fund created by your agency that allows donors to make a gift to the fund and receive market income for one or two lives. While receiving life income, the donor commits his or her remainder interests to your agency. Covering the expense of the operation of a pooled income fund, however, generally requires aggregate giving of $100,000 or more.

Will

A legal document directing the transfer of one's property after death.

References

Chapter 1: Creating a Strong Fund-Raising Organization
1. R. Ensman, "Setting Priorities in the Small Shop," *Fund Raising Management*, November 1988.

Chapter 2: How to Develop a Fund-Raising Board
1. David Emenhiser, "Power Influence and Contributions: What Every Fund Raiser Should Know About Power Structures," *NSFRE Journal*, Spring 1991.
2. Brian O'Connell, "Fund Raising," *Nonprofit Management Series.* (Washington, D.C.: Independent Sector, 1988).
3. David Emenhiser, "Power Influence and Contributions: What Every Fund Raiser Should Know About Power Structures," *NSFRE Journal*, Spring 1991.

Adapted from Mengerink, W. C. "Asking for Outright Gifts: A Challenge for Human Service Agencies." *Fund Raising Institute Monthly Portfolio*, June 1991.

Chapter 3: Developing A Major Gifts Program
1. W. C. Mengerink, "Management with Muscle: Strengthening Your Bottom Line," *Management Review*, July 1990.
2. The Taft Group, *Fund Raiser's Guide to Private Fortunes*, 2d ed. (Rockville, MD: The Taft Group).

Chapter 4: Developing an Annual Fund

1. P. H. Schneiter and D. T. Nelson, *The Thirteen Most Common Fund Raising Mistakes and How to Avoid Them* (Rockville, MD: The Taft Group, 1982).

Chapter 5: The Zen of Grantsmanship

1. S. D. Hicks, ed., *Fund Raiser's Guide to Human Service Funding (Rockville, MD: The Taft Group).*

2. N. J. Kiritz, "Program Planning and Proposal Writing," *The Grantsmanship News Reprint,* 1974.

3. Ralph Brody, *Problem Solving: Concepts and Methods for Community Organizations,* (New York: Human Sciences Press, Inc., 1982).

Adapted from W. C. Mengerink, "The Zen of Grantsmanship." *Grassroots Fund Raising Journal,* Summer 1990.

Chapter 6: Corporate Philanthropy: An Oxymoron?

1. W. C. Mengerink, "Management with Muscle: Strengthening Your Bottom Line," *Management Review,* July 1990.

Chapter 9: How to Conduct a Capital Campaign

1. P. H. Schneiter and D. T. Nelson, *The Thirteen Most Common Fund Raising Mistakes and How to Avoid Them,* (Rockville, MD: The Taft Group, 1982).

Adapted from W. C. Mengerink, "How to Conduct a Capital Campaign and Live to Tell About It." *The Grassroots Fund Raising Journal,* August 1989.

Chapter 10: Burn, Burned, Burnt: The Conjugation of a Fund Raiser

1. R. Woolfolk and F. Richardson, *Stress, Sanity & Survival* (New York: The New American Library, Inc., 1978).

Adapted from W. C. Mengerink, "Burn, Burned, Burnt: The Conjugation of a Fund Raiser." *Fund Raising Management,* April 1990.

Suggested Reading

Ashton, D., *The Complete Guide to Planned Giving*, 2d ed. Cambridge, Massachusetts: JLA Publications, 1991. In my experience, the most frequently suggested guide for planned giving.

Brody, R., *Problem Solving: Concepts and Methods for Community Organizations*, New York: Human Sciences Press, 1982. Provides a road map for developing problem statements and objectives for proposal writing.

Hicks, S. D., ed., *Fund Raiser's Guide to Human Service Funding*, Rockville, MD: The Taft Group. An excellent resource for social or human service agencies doing grant research.

Ensman, R., "Setting Priorities in the Small Shop." *Fund Raising Management.*, November 1988. A concise description of the challenges of doing first things first.

Lautman, K. P. and Goldstein, H., *Dear Friend: Mastering the Art of Direct Mail Fund Raising.*, 2d ed. Rockville, MD: The Taft Group, 1991. Contains everything you need to know about direct mail fund raising.

Lord, J. G., The Raising of Money: Thirty-five Essentials Every Trustee Should Know. Cleveland: Third Sector Press, 1984. One of the better books on board development and relationships.

Schneiter, P. H. and Nelson D. T., *The Thirteen Most Common Fund Raising Mistakes and How to Avoid Them.* Rockville, MD: The

Taft Group, 1982. This was recommended to me eight years ago as the best in its class and I agree.

Seltzer, M., *Securing Your Organization's Future*. New York: The Foundation Center, 1987. Provides a broad overview of the whole field of development and planning.

Strunk, W., Jr., and White, E. B. *The Elements of Style.*, 3d ed. New York: Macmillan, 1979. The best book on writing I can recommend.

Index